"Bob Mounce has provided a
of short essays (blogs really)
think about some of the famc
sumptions of society. He poke:
offers the readers new perspectives in ways
ideas that will bless."

—JIM SINGLETON
Associate Professor of Pastoral Leadership and Evangelism,
Gordon-Conwell Theological Seminary, South Hamilton, MA

"It takes a lifetime to accrue the kind of wisdom my ninety-three-
year-old friend, Bob Mounce, has gleaned . . . and it's what makes this
respected Christian leader a true sage of our time! When Bob speaks,
I listen. I encourage you to do the same as you peruse this special
book you hold in your hands. For when it comes to passing along
favorite 'sayings,' not every familiar quote is worth repeating. Thank
you, Bob, for bringing common sense and biblical clarity to what
others say in the kingdom of Christ!"

—JONI EARECKSON TADA
Joni and Friends International Disability Center, Agoura Hills, CA

SO THEY SAY

SO THEY SAY

ROBERT H. MOUNCE

RESOURCE *Publications* · Eugene, Oregon

SO THEY SAY

Resource Publications
An Imprint of Wipf and Stock Publishers
199 W. 8th Ave., Suite 3
Eugene, OR 97401

www.wipfandstock.com

ISBN 13: 978-1-4982-0166-7

Manufactured in the U.S.A.   09/30/2014

Contents

Contents

Contents

Preface

I'VE ALWAYS LOVED A good quotation. It condenses so much wisdom into so few words. In fact, I like to read short books. It seems to me that almost anything can be said with fewer words. It was John Calvin, a primary figure in the Protestant Reformation, who coined the phrase "lucid brevity." I will try to follow my own advice in this preface.

A long time ago a friend of mine, well equipped to speak on the subject, said that progress in science is nothing more than finding order in confusion. In science one begins with a mass of data. Observation of the data hopefully brings a clue as to how one might handle it. For instance, drop a ball 100 times and it always hits the ground. Aha! The law of gravity is discovered. And so it goes. That set me to thinking about language. When the concept is not clear, it presents itself as little more than verbal data—complexity with no unifying principle. Then, someone gets it. The data is put into a meaningful relationship and out comes a pithy quotation. For example: the opposition is fierce, our forces are weak, we want to win but question our strength, what should be my choice in the face of defeat—"Give Me Liberty Or Give Me Death." The birth of a quotation is clarity out of confusion.

So I started paying attention to quotes, not in the huge anthologies conveniently arranged by subject or author, but those that you run onto rather accidentally. Many came from reading, others from conversation. What attracted me was the opportunity they provided for reaction, sometimes positively, other times in opposition—it didn't make any difference. My reactions came from my own understanding of reality that, in turn, has been conditioned by a Christian upbringing. It is my worldview. When I object to a clever statement by Mr. Somebody I want it to show

how I see the issue from a Christian worldview. My intention is not to put someone down. Perhaps the majority of the quotations in this book are one with which I agree—well, for the most part. My efforts are to challenge, support, alter slightly, or to enhance the quote. I apologize to the person quoted realizing that they will probably not have the chance to respond.

So what you have in this little book is a series of good quotations and my reflections on them. May the quotes themselves, and hopefully my responses, stir you to think about the subjects addressed. I wish you a good journey into an exercise that I have found intriguing. Few things would please me more than to incite a reaction from you!

Robert Mounce

How do you prove what doesn't exist?

FRIEDRICH NIETZSCHE IS OFTEN quoted as saying, "There are no facts, only interpretations." The German philosopher is of such intellectual stature that we have no option but to pay attention to what he has to say. He is asking us to accept as a "fact" that there are no facts. But wait a minute. Isn't he expecting us to accept that very assertion as a fact? Or is he saying that it is simply a true statement? But isn't a true statement a fact? For the life of me I can't see how you can do away with facts and then make a factual statement about what doesn't exist.

There are undoubtedly the philosophically minded who can point out the fallacy of my inability to see his point — and your comments are welcomed. But for the time being my problem with the non-existence of reality remains. There are very few, if any, who can argue persuasively for a form of metaphysical nihilism that denies its own existence.

The Judeo-Christian world-view begins with a God who created the universe as we know it. We accept its existence because we can touch it, taste it, smell it, weigh it, etc. We consider its existence a fact, and so also the One who created it. Granted, we can interpret that fact in various ways, but our interpretation doesn't alter the reality of the fact.

"So what," you may say. And I can see your point. Most of us just don't live in the lofty world of philosophical musing. However, with the "loss of reality" goes the loss of responsibility (there is no one to be responsible to) and civil life as we know it disintegrates. The end of that road is raw savagery. To deny reality is to remove the basis for all moral codes.

Simplicity, the ultimate sophistication

I'M ATTRACTED BY SIMPLICITY. Not the simplicity that has never considered an issue, but the simplicity that emerges from careful consideration. It is what *Oliver Wendell Holmes* called "the simplicity on the other side of complexity." Problems begin in a haze of uncertainty and normally become more complex before the light begins to dawn. So I'm not advocating an uniformed simplicity but the simplicity that emerges from genuine involvement with the issue.

Simplicity is an important goal in a number of realms of life. For instance, although few in contemporary American culture have adopted it, there is a certain beauty in the simple life style. I'm not talking about poverty, but the decision to live simply so that time, energy, and resources can be spent on things that matter. I have a son who refuses to be caught up in the gotta-have-it mentality. He holds that "whatever you own, owns you," and the more I think about it, the more I think he's absolutely correct.

Then there is simplicity in design. John Maeda, president of the Rhode Island School of Design, is widely known for his emphasis on "Designing for Simplicity." Apple's success stems in large part from Steve Job's commitment to simplicity in design. It's been said that a work of art is not finished until there is nothing left that can be taken away. The point is best made with Leonardo da Vinci's conclusion that "simplicity is the ultimate sophistication."

On a very practical level there is what we might call simplicity in communication. There are very few things that can't be said more effectively with fewer words (including this blog). A convincing speaker evades unnecessary verbiage and makes his point in an easily remembered phrase, e.g., "tax the rich." Have you ever noticed that a common tactic in a "debate" is the claim that "It isn't as simple as that." The insistence on complexity comes from a personal need to confuse the issue.

I agree with Confucius that "life is really simple, but we insist on making it complicated." As a Christian believer approaching his 93rd birthday, I see with clarity that the only critical issue in this brief moment we call life is preparation for eternity. All that seems to have absorbed our energies and time suddenly becomes beside the point. Who was it that, on the scaffold, said, " Depend up on it, sir, when a man knows he is to be hanged in a fortnight, it concentrates his mind wonderfully?" I'm not suggesting that we abandon intellectual pursuits, but that we maintain a priority that prevents the inconsequential, with all its confusion and complexity, to replace the simplicity of that which has eternal significance.

Why higher education got lower

THERE WAS A DAY when higher education was, as the label suggests, higher. Students went to college to be immersed in an intellectual environment structured around the best that man has said and done since the beginning of reflective thought. The academy existed to discuss ideas, not to provide instructions on how to do something. Those were the golden years of western civilization. Scholars were the ones who encouraged thought and guided it toward goals still in the process of being defined. School was a place for discussion; in fact, the word "school" comes from the Greek *schole*, "spare time, idleness, a place where leisure is employed for discussion." People didn't go to school to be taught something but to discuss something.

The noted Irish poet, *William Butler Yeats*, would agree. By the time of his death in 1939, American higher education was beginning to look like a vast training program for the industrial world. As a corrective against that direction, Yeats reminded his generation that "education is not the filling of a pail but the lighting of a fire." For the Nobel winning poet (in literature, 1923) that may seem like an unimpressive aside, but not so. He believed the important issues of life would not be solved by science but by poets able to speak simply. Were he with us today he would be shocked to see the extent to which "pail filling" has replaced serious discussion of concerns that determine the direction of civilization.

And why is it that this mentality has become dominant in our institutions of "higher" education? Could it be that in the short run knowing how to do something is more profitable than trying to understand those issues which in the long run will prove to be significant? We all know that at the moment a young graduate in philosophy may well find himself asking, "Where is the food stamp line?" I feel sorry for those who for a time may have to work at minimum wage or lower, but I feel worse for those who give up the excitement of learning (the "fire" that needs to be lit) for the benefit of having all that doesn't satisfy anyway.

As members of the biological class called mammals there is nothing we do (with one exception) that is not done far more proficiently by some animal. A shark's olfactory ability is so great that it can "smell" blood in the water miles away. Setting aside for this particular discussion the theological proposition that man is made in the image of God (I believe it), man is distinguished from other mammals only by an advanced capacity for thought. His frontal lobe is significantly larger and infinitely more complex. Higher education should "set it on fire" by focusing it on issues central to life.

Can you doubt faith but not doubt doubt?

ALFRED LORD TENNYSON NOTED, and I accept it — although not without certain reservations — that, "there lives more faith in honest doubt, believe me, than in half the creeds." It all sounds so intellectually correct. "Check your sources" is the mantra of the academy. And you should. Especially in the age of the Internet, nothing should automatically be accepted as true (even Snopes!). Truth seems to be increasingly elusive. In the first edition of my commentary on Revelation I wrote, to my chagrin, that Antipas was roasted to death in a "brazen bull" (p. 97). That's what all the scholars writing on the Apocalypse said. Then it was discovered that the place of martyrdom was a "brazen bowl" (see 2nd edition, p. 80.) Even though I had written "bull" (in the 1st edition) I never could actually picture a person being roasted in an animal, but that's what the authorities said.

So doubt plays a genuine role in scholarship and life itself. But when you check the use of "doubt/doubted/doubting" in the NT you will repeatedly find statements like, "If you have faith and do not doubt" you can move mountains (Mark 11:23) and, "When you ask, you must believe and not doubt" (James 1:6). I was unable to find a single statement in scripture that encouraged doubt.

Hmmmmm. What now? Since truth by definition does not contradict itself, there must be a tertium quid (a third way) that embraces both. Tennyson is right (I believe) and so also is God (if I am allowed to put it that way). In the realm of possible verification, doubt will clarify and serve to direct us to truth. But in the significantly larger realm, where the rules of intellectual verification are inadequate, faith calls on us to believe. Doubt becomes inconsistent with faith. My mind always goes back to that Old Testament invitation, "Taste and see that the Lord is good" (Psalm

34:8). In spiritual matters the "seeing" (the understanding) always follows the "tasting" (the act of faith). Doubt may hinder the decision but not the result. I tasted the Lord and can tell you without the shadow of a doubt that he is "good."

Why big is not better

SOMEONE NOTED THAT PEOPLE are like manure: Spread out over the land they do a lot of good, but piled together they smell. I think that the ultimate pile is probably any oversized government — piled high in some tax-funded building it does what it does best, the wrong thing. *George Washington* put it bluntly: "Government is not reason, it is not eloquence, it is force; like fire, a troublesome servant and a fearful master. "

Several points deserve discussion; first, that government is certainly not reason. I can't think of any reasonable person racking up a debt that his progeny will have to pay, or forcing on his children an untried and questionable wellness program they don't want, or doing away with locks on the doors in hopes that the local thugs will become nice people. Such unilateral decisions are not reasonable, except, of course, in terms of personal benefit. The abuse of power is the central malfeasance of mankind, the most common expression of universal narcissism. Secondly, government is certainly not eloquence, that is, good government. The lofty expression of mutual goals is harmless in itself but what a nation needs is steady, sensible, realistic progress toward broadly accepted goals.

What Washington said is exactly right: government is power — the larger the bureaucracy, the greater the power. Obviously, leadership is necessary in a civilized society, but the power it provides keeps expanding at an increasing rate until it gains absolute ascendancy. Since government is power, it needs desperately to be held in check, the sooner the better.

Of special interest to me are Washington's two descriptive phrases describing power. First, like fire it is a "troublesome servant." Instead of carrying out the will of the master, it acts on its own. Theoretically, it should serve those who need its help, provide strength for those who falter, and safeguard the gains of yesterday's struggle. But it is far more apt to do the opposite — instead of helping it corrupts. Everyone knows Lord Acton's famous remark, "Power tends to corrupt and complete power corrupts completely." It is truly a "troublesome servant." And it is also a "fearful master." Anyone familiar with history knows that from the time of the Roman emperors such as Tiberius and Caligula to today's Hitlers and Pol Pots, power has expressed itself in unbelievable cruelty. Power holds the opportunity for the greatest good but on a regular basis results in the greatest evil. Scripture teaches that government was established by God (Rom 13:1-7) and to rebel against a governing authority is to rebel against God (vs. 2). Yet, that ideal is regularly perverted by sinful man, and power "corrupts completely."

Our founding fathers understood this, and devised a system of social regulation to counter the abuse of power. It is never to be lodged in one branch of government. This limitation on power has resulted in the birth and growth of what is certainly the most remarkable and productive nation in the world. Long live the use and control of this otherwise "fearful master."

Don't waste the irreplaceable

DWIGHT EISENHOWER ONCE NOTED, "Wise men do not lie down on the tracks of history waiting for the train of the future to run over them." Vivid metaphor, and more true than we are normally willing to admit. It is self-evident that to each of us was given a certain amount of time and how it is used is strictly up to the individual. Time is the only irreplaceable element in life. An hour once used, for whatever purpose, is gone and cannot be regained.

How we use time is an expression of our priorities in life. For some, life is all about achieving our goals. For many the primary purpose in life seems to be the acquisition of stuff. Why else would we carve out a schedule in which "time on the job" is the central concern? That orientation is widely acknowledged for the earlier years in a profession, after all, the house needs to be purchased, the kids need a good education, etc. All laudable concerns, but when is enough, enough? What seems to happen is that our desire for more morphs from an understandable concern to an addiction that controls he rest of life. This makes time simply something to be filled with doing, rather than an opportunity to enjoy the fruit of energy wisely spent.

For others, time is little else than an endless occasion to do whatever we want to do. This outlook is prevalent in a certain sector of society and has the same potential as above for abusing time. Little expected, nothing required. For most people, this would be a contradiction of all that it means to be alive and well in time. It is hard to convince the average person that life has no significant purpose and that God, if there be one, is unconcerned whether or not we squander time however we want to.

Somewhere between these extremes there ought to be the balance the yields the most productive and most satisfactory way to use the gift of time. But where is that balance, the fulcrum between work and play, earning and enjoying? Here is one possibility: Genesis shows how God apportioned his time during the one week in which he is said to have worked (speaking anthropomorphically) — he worked six days and took a day off (Gen 2:2-3). Not a bad idea. Good ratio. Work a solid day, relax, do something entirely different, in the evening. Work in your profession 40 years, and then retire. Mingle "work" and "recreation."

Now there is an interesting word, "recreation;" it means to "create anew," to "re-freshen." So there is a definite purpose in not working a reasonable amount of time; it is to renew, refresh, recondition, reinvigorate. A period of renewal is a gift we give to ourselves. Jesus taught that "the Sabbath was made for man, not man for the Sabbath" (Mark 2:27). It is as true in the secular world as it is for the community of faith. Time off restores, revives.

So, do what God did. Balance your time in successive periods of work and relaxation. And do both intentionally with all the effort required.

Is it summer or winter inside?

Do you ever read a quotation that makes you feel good but you're not exactly sure why it does? That's how I felt when I read *Camus'* "In the depth of winter, I finally learned that within me there lay an invincible summer." We have come to expect such memorable statements from the French philosopher and writer who in 1957, was awarded the Nobel Prize for Literature. To translate his insight into less poetic terms, what I hear is, "When things get really bad, I find within my self a bright hope for tomorrow." Very uplifting. We've all known bad times and quite often what we've felt to be tragic at the moment turned out far better than we could have expected.

My problem with that somewhat rosy scenario is that so often it doesn't work out. It has not been my experience that every difficult situation has been solved by a new and fresh realization rising from within that convinces a better tomorrow. Many winter storms turn out to be less severe than expected, but not because of an "invincible summer" which lies within. In my experience the storms of life are a very real part of life itself and are not melted by a warm summer sun which I possess. That which overcomes the current difficulty doesn't seem to lie within me. I question not that a strong sense of optimism won't deal with difficulty better than despair, but matters of the soul require help that will reach way deeper into the problem.

The prophet Jeremiah wrote, "The human heart is the most deceitful of all things, and desperately wicked. Who really knows how bad it is?" (17:9) I would ask, "Does the wicked heart contain an 'invincible summer' as well?"

Perhaps this is not a Yes or No question. Those that accept the Bible as authoritative must of necessity agree to what it says. But in a larger context, is that all it says? I think not. Fallen we are (Read Genesis 3 and Romans 3) but we were created in God's image (Gen 1:27). That means there is real hope for a coming summer. It was God's intent that his offspring return to Eden, and for that purpose he gave his Son as the necessary price for redemption. Now that is the real spring!

Does the Spirit still inspire?

IN DISCUSSING HIS BOOK, *Killing Jesus, Bill O'Reilly* commented that he was "inspired by the Holy Spirit." It caused a flood of reactionary emails. I tend to think that those wishing to correct him thought that he said that the Holy Spirit told him *what* to write rather than telling him *to* write. On one hand, Christians who take the Bible seriously believe that the Spirit inspired the writers in the sense that they were told what to write. However, we often speak of being inspired in the sense of being strongly moved by a force from the outside. Certainly, Martin Luther Jr's "I had a Dream" speech was inspired in this sense (although some might claim that the Holy Spirit was speaking through him.)

I bring this up only because the other night, I felt inspired. I was sitting at the piano looking out to the West across the Sound at a remarkably beautiful sunset. It was deeply moving. I thought, God must really love beauty because there is so much of it in the world. The line came to me, "I see your love of beauty in the sunset." Deciding to take it a step further I added, "I feel your awesome power in every storm." At that point I began to wonder whether I could write a verse of poetry. After a pause I wrote in my mind, "I hear your voice through nature's wonders" (I've always marveled at God's self revelation in nature — see Romans 1:19-20). About that time an experience came to mind — a homily I had heard in an Episcopal Church some 10-15 years ago. The point was that in the presentation of the biblical story of God's great redemptive act, instead of starting with an emphasis on man's sinfulness as a result of his fall, we need to begin the story at the real beginning — man free from sin in the Garden of Eden, walking and talking with God. So, I added a fourth line, "Calling, 'Child, dear child, Oh come back home.'" God's voice comes to us through nature, calling us back home to Eden. Question: was I inspired, or not? You can certainly improve on the verse, but the experience of writing it was unique. In fact, I wrote four more verses to carry out the theme. I am going to include the lyrics and you are the judge.

The Grand Old Story

I see your love of beauty in the sunset;
I feel your awesome power in every storm.
I hear your voice thru nature's wonders,
Calling, "Child, dear child, Oh come back home."

Once in Eden free from sin;
We walked with God and talked with him.
No joy withheld, one tree denied.
"No harm can come," the Temper lied.

Lost in sin, we wandered in vain,
Longing for love, to be forgiven again.
Then, down came the Son from heaven above,
God's atonement for sin, the proof of his love.

"Look up my child, the price it has been paid.
Come stand by my side while sin 's victories fade.
Your faith is the key to heaven above;
It's broken sin's grip, there is freedom in love."

We see your love of beauty in the sunset.
We feel your awesome power in every storm.
We've heard your voice thru Gospel's story.
We're back in Eden, our eternal home.

Robert Mounce

Is faith irrational?

"THE CONFIDENCE PEOPLE HAVE in their beliefs is not a measure of the quality of evidence but of the coherence of the story that the mind has managed to construct." So says the Nobel-winning psychologist *Daniel Kahneman*. That means people are more, or less, confident in their religious preference (be it Christian, Buddhist, Islamic, or Seventh Day Adventist for that matter) depending on how that belief system fits into an existing mind-set. For example, if you grew up in a highly secularized family you would probably find Christ with his miracles more difficult to accept than Buddha who reportedly possessed superhuman powers but said of miracles, "I dislike, reject and despise them." It would be more coherent with the story your mind has constructed.

The problem with this is that it makes belief a rational product. We believe because it seems to fit the larger story that has been put together piece by piece on the basis of coherence. All this seems to be an apple/orange problem. Something is rational if it does not offend what the mind assumes to be an acceptable pattern. If the car won't start we will have to find some other way to go to the store. It makes sense. It is some how related to the real world as we experience it.

Belief systems by definition (and here is the orange) lie outside those narrow boundaries. Belief relates to that which offers no quick guarantee of authenticity. We don't believe, what has always been obvious, we know it. But people do believe (most people, that is) that there is a superhuman being, some force, out there that somehow oversees what we call reality. There is nothing in our tangible world that supplies the necessary coherence that Dr. Kahneman calls for. I am not suggesting that belief is irrational, only that it should not be reduced to some artificial prerequisite that we manufacture. Many years ago a professor of theology, E. J. Carnell, defined faith as "the resting of the mind in the sufficiency of the evidence." We arrive at a conclusion because the evidence leads us in that direction — although it never fully arrives. So coherence does have a place in belief but is not the sole arbiter of what we should or should not belief.

Can "force" reveal itself?

ALBERT EINSTEIN WROTE THAT if you "try and penetrate with our limited means the secrets of nature . . . you will find that, behind all the discernible concatenations, there remains something subtle, intangible and inexplicable. Veneration for this force beyond anything that we can comprehend is my religion. To that extent I am, in point of fact, religious."

The apostle Paul wrote, "Since the creation of the world, God's invisible qualities — his eternal power and divine nature — have been clearly seen, being understood from what has been made" (Rom 1:20).

Both references are to what theology calls general revelation. While Einstein recognized only the "force" behind nature, Paul correctly identified it [him] as God. Biblical theology teaches that with the coming of Christ, general revelation has been supplemented by special revelation. Through creation God revealed his existence; through Christ he revealed his love. The incarnation is God invading his own creation and through Christ reconciling the world to himself (2 Corinthians 5:19). Nature reveals the "eternal power" and "divine nature" of God; the incarnation is a demonstration of his love. He revealed himself as redemptive love by sending his Son as the necessary sacrifice for sin. A correct translation of the Greek *houtos* in John 3:16 makes the verse read, "For this is how God loved the world: he gave his one and only Son . . . " Now that is special!

Are there mountains too high to climb?

"THE QUESTION ISN'T WHO is going to let me; it's who is going to stop me." Sounds like the proud boast of the young bravado about to storm the castle to rescue fair maiden. We admire the dauntless courage of the hero taking on the impossible task, unwilling to be cowered by overwhelming opposition. But the quotation is from *Ayn Rand*, the Russian/American novelist, play writer, philosopher, best known by most for her novel *Atlas Shrugged*. Like every pronouncement of this sort, its validity depends on context. Here is one that makes the quotation look really good.

I know a young man who after several years of substandard grades in college decided he wanted a degree after all. The registrar said, "Take another semester and get your grade average up to B," not an easy thing to do, given three years of work significantly below that level. He studied diligently and earned almost all A's, but it still didn't bring the grade average up to the mark. At this point they wouldn't "let him," but could they "stop him?" That was the question. He said No, beat down the doors, pled his cause, got another chance and graduated, not *summa cum laude* but on the president's list for his final year. Ayn, you are exactly right — they wouldn't let him but they couldn't stop him. And we admire that kind of vigorous approach to life.

But is the theorem universally applicable? Is it wise, in certain situations, not to challenge opposition? And of course the answer is, "Yes." Common sense tells us that. In the real world there are "mountains too high to climb" and "oceans too wide to swim." Speaking to the crowds, Jesus said, "What king marching to war against another king would not first sit down and consider whether with ten thousand men he could stand up to the other who was advancing against him with twenty thousand?" (Luke 14:31)

So everything depends upon context. The who-can-stop-me mentality is praiseworthy when the goal is worthy (even though it might require enormous personal effort), but foolish when the goal has no particular value. Sometimes the impossible is challenged for nothing more than the supposed approval others. And that's sad. Personal worth is the result of doing what is worthy, not of conjuring up ways to make others think so. When opposition is faced, it is wise to consider not only the cost but also the importance of that which is pursued. Don Quixote's quest to revive chivalry was romantic, but Sancho Panza, his squire had a better grip on reality.

Progress versus expansion

I KNOW IT'S NOT fair to pick on an idea that is down and out (theoretically, that is), but there is one organizational system that keeps expanding anyway — bureaucracy. Talk about resiliency: *Einstein* calls it "the death of all sound work," *Chris Salcedo* defines it as "the art of making the possible impossible," and it's portrayed as a new game sweeping the country in which everyone stands in a circle and the first person to do anything loses. The term, but not the concept, goes back to the German sociologist *Max Weber* who held that the ideal bureaucracy was a hierarchical organization with clearly delineated lines of authority and a set of regulations that would answer every possible exigency.

Most scholars who work in the field acknowledge that bureaucracy may be technically superior to other forms of organizational theory but recognize that the human element makes it ineffective in the long run. Even Weber saw it as a threat to individual freedom and feared that it could lead to a "polar night of icy darkness." Let's look at how bureaucracy works in our own democratic system.

Every bureaucratic system seems to have the incredible ability to grow no matter what. In fact, growth appears to be its major purpose. As academic dean in a state university I found myself at budget time looking for ways to spend unallocated money so next year's budget wouldn't be reduced. There is nothing wrong with growth except that isn't the purpose of an educational institution (at least that kind of growth.) Further, the larger and more complex a bureaucracy becomes, the less able it is to get something done. There are too many levels of oversight that must give their okay to even the simplest task. And that costs time and dollars better spent elsewhere.

Then there is a certain loss of individuality that accompanies bureaucracy. The very structure discourages creativity and innovation. It's hard to move ahead with an idea if that idea must be okayed by a hierarchy of professional managers who may or may not have any interest in the contribution you wish to make. It's nobody's fault, just the way the system works. Bureaucracy creates its own jobs. Relatively insignificant agencies in the federal government have double or triple the number of employees than would be required by the private sector for the same task. While the current health care act is 960 pages in length, the necessary regulations (as compared to the bill) run 30 to 1, or some 11,588,500 words. That is a monumental task even for a bureaucracy!

In the final analysis bureaucracy is the organizational expression of a world-view that tends to place the welfare of the group over that of the individual. It runs contrary to the Christian emphasis on the supreme importance of the individual, made in the image of God created to live in a vital relationship with others but not under the supposed superiority of the group.

Where do you want to go?

IT IS CRYSTAL CLEAR that society is changing. Perhaps it always has but most informed observers tell us that the change in America during the last 50 years is significantly greater than in any previous time in history. So, if in fact we are changing, it may be well to take a look at where we are going.

Many would claim that we're headed in the wrong direction. Eric Blair, the English writer we know as *George Orwell*, apparently felt that we had hit bottom. He said, "We have now sunk to a depth at which restatement of the obvious is the first duty of intelligent men." Nothing can be accomplished until society recognizes it has been going in the wrong direction. Change itself is not progress. Progress means getting closer to where you want to be. More often than not it involves a radical change in direction. To step backward after making a wrong turn is actually moving forward. *C S Lewis* writes that progress is to turn-about when walking in the wrong direction, and that "the man who turns back soonest is the most progressive man." (*Mere Christianity*)

What is abundantly clear is that progress is impossible without a goal. If you don't know where you're going you will never get there. However, as a society we do not reflect on this crucial issue very often. There seems to be a scattered consensus that as a nation we would be better off if everyone could live more comfortably — have a better house, more expensive car, more money for things we want, etc. And the energies of many are directed toward that goal. Others have, for all practical purposes, dropped out of the race and are content to live on what happens to come their way.

My point of view is that as a society we are not finding contentment, not making progress toward something that provides satisfaction and builds a sense of self-worth, because we are headed in the wrong direction. When we make it to the top after a life time of strenuous involvement with the requirements of success, there is little or nothing of worth waiting for us. Of course, the Christian faith speaks directly to this issue. Knowing that there was no reasonable answer, Jesus asked, "What benefit is there if you gain the whole world but lose your own soul?" (Matthew 16:26) Man was not created simply to accumulate stuff. In the deep recesses of his soul he finds no lasting satisfaction in anything short of fulfilling a spiritual destiny. God created us for fellowship with himself, so ultimately the only authentic progress is to move toward him.

I am aware that this sounds like a sermon, but it is intended as a valid observation about life. In my contacts throughout the last 90 plus years, it has been those people who have had the highest respect for the spiritual dimension of life who are most content and at peace with reality. No one has put it more succinctly than the French polymath, *Blaise Pascal*, who wrote, "There is a God shaped vacuum in the heart of every man which cannot be filled by any created thing, but only by God, the Creator, made known through Jesus." Goals exist to provide direction in life. The ultimate question is, "Where do you want to go?

The art of kissing

MARQUIS DE VAUVENARGUES WAS of the opinion that "When a thought is too weak to be expressed simply, it should be rejected." Ambiguity in simple prose is the result of the author's failure to think clearly on the issue he is writing about, expecting the reader to clarify the issue. Among the naive this may come through as profound; among the nature it is recognized as intellectual weakness. After a lifetime of serious theological thought, Karl Barth told us that the essence of biblical revelation was, "Jesus loves me, this I know; for the Bible tells me so." KISS (Keep It Simple, Stupid) is still the motto of those not ashamed to summarize their better thoughts in language that conveys. In his introduction to his commentary on Romans, John Calvin said that the best thing an interpreter can do is to make the meaning of the text clear and to do it with as few words as possible. He called it "lucid brevity." Hopefully that is why this little piece is so short.

The sine qua non of friendship

IT IS INTERESTING THAT while disparate world-views see the larger picture quite differently, a given quotation can often fit comfortably in both. For instance, Mencius a famous Chinese philosopher of the third century BC and a principal interpreter of Confucianism, believed in the unique goodness of the individual and that bad moral character was the result of society's failure to exercise a positive influence on the individual. That is quite distinct from the historic Judeo-Christian position that man, although created in the image of God, chose to sin — the result of which was a basic flaw in human nature. Yet the Christian can agree wholeheartedly with *Mencius* that, "friendship is one mind in two bodies."

World-views can be diagrammed as large overlapping circles. A number of ideals may be distinct to one or the other but at the same time there exist many that are common to both. As you would expect, issues that are central to a world-view determine where they stand in the diagram. Human nature is certainly one of them. Mencius believed that negative qualities in a person were the influence of society while the Christian faith teaches that, "it is from within, out of a person's heart, that evil thoughts come — sexual immorality, theft, murder." (Mark 7:21).

But, back to the quotation, "Friendship is one mind in two bodies." It is shared values that draw people together, especially when those values are religious or political. To disagree in those areas keeps any relationship nominal at best. At the same time there is such a wide range of common acceptance that individuals who hold fundamentally different principles are able to live in harmony and share a common life. While I may not agree with a man who honestly believes that government is the answer for society's ills, there is no reason that I cannot enjoy a good football game or a good dinner with him. One of the goals of a democratic civilization should be to maintain a pleasant working relationship with all others of this broad point of view. It is only when one ideology attempts to force its point of view on others who are not persuaded, that serious conflict results. Unfortunately there are so many examples of this in today's world. One would be the atheist's concern that God have no place in discussions in the public square. Since the majority does believes in God, it would seem unfair to penalize them because a small minority claims to be offended. Of course the rights of that minority must be honored but not to the extent that the rights of the majority are over-ruled.

Genuine friendship is a wonderful relationship. I would hope that a respectful relationship between those of differing ideals can exist as well. A major step toward that goal is to treat the other as we would have the other treat us. Of course that is what the New Testament teaches as the Golden Rule.

Careful with words!

MARGARET THATCHER ONCE WROTE that to her "consensus seems to be the process of abandoning all beliefs, principles, values and policies. So it is something in which no one believes and to which no one objects." No wonder she earned the title "Iron Lady"! Many would hold that consensus is the guiding principle of informed society. Isn't that how people work together for the common good?

Giving her the latitude that comes with her "seems to be," it is still remarkable that a major player in the Western world (Prime Minister of the United Kingdom from 1979 to 1990) would call into question a principle so widely accepted.

So what's the problem (if there is one) with consensus? It depends upon what one means by the word. Most often "consensus" is used to denote the opinion of the majority. Two groups meet and, after discussion, release a "consensus opinion" that they will follow plan A rather than plan B. But the more basic meaning of the word is "general agreement or concord." To have a consensus means to be in agreement. That is different. Dr. Thatcher's concern was that people of differing persuasions often abandon their principles to arrive at what seems to be a "workable solution." On a given subject, two political parties may well share a common goal but differ on how to achieve it. If they discuss the issue in an open and honest manner, both sides may come to see some practical insight on how best to solve the problem. Then, if they adjust their approach somewhat, they have not compromised their principles but have reached a consensus on how to arrive where they both want to be.

Since the beginning of time, people of principal have brought stability to society. They could be counted on to do exactly what they said. I believe in firmness in principle but flexibility in process.

How to prevent the inevitable

THE OTHER EVENING DR. *Phil* reminded one of his guests, "You can't unring a bell." Once the clapper hits the bell, that's it. There is no way to stop the ring. Actions inevitably have consequences. We all recognize the truth of this in our everyday world. Touch a hot stove and you burn your finger. But when it comes to the world of relationships, we tend to act as though consequentiality doesn't exist.

Why is that? Why do we keep doing what experience has clearly shown to produce the same unwanted result. Do we hope that next time it will be different? Perhaps 2 + 2 will = 5 . . . next time. I don't think that's the answer. We know that excessive speed will, in time, end up in an accident or a traffic fine. But we exceed the posted speed limit anyway.

I think we ignore the law of cause and effect because we want so desperately to do whatever it is. Consequence doesn't matter.

"Go ahead and have the extra drink; don't remind me how gruesome an accident on the road can be.

"Pass on the bit of gossip you've heard; don't make me think about integrity being undermined by passing on information damaging to another.

"Check out the questionable picture on the internet; at the moment I don't care about the life-destroying power of addiction. I'm going to go ahead and do it because I want to."

We know it will never bring any lasting satisfaction but we do it anyway. Desire dominates and we lunge forward. However, there is an alternative to failure. The bell won't ring unless it is struck. The unwanted consequence won't happen unless the action is taken. We understand that intellectually, but insight seems always to be trumped by desire. The missing ingredient so far is volitional — nothing less than the internal strength to say No. For the Christian, that strength is provided by the abiding presence of the Spirit. However, even then his help must be requested.

To fix or not to fix?

IT WAS QUITE SOME time ago that *Mark Twain,* the American author and humorist, wrote "If you don't read the newspaper you are uninformed; if you do read the newspaper you are misinformed." In 1910, the year of his death, television would have been considered a pipe dream. If he were writing today he would probably put it something like this, "If you don't watch TV you won't know whose dancing with the stars; and if you read the blogs you won't have the slightest idea what is true and what isn't."

I went to Snopes the other day to find out what they thought about a certain story circulating on the Internet and discovered that over two-thirds of the material regarding the president was false. It seems as though once a person takes a position on a political issue, all evidence is regarded as true or false on the basis of whether or not it supports that opinion. What I am seeing is a breakdown of rational discussion, especially on issues of genuine significance. Someone said that "truth is the first victim of war" and that is true both on the battlefield and in national debate. Facts are "true" only if they are helpful in winning one's point.

I am in no way hesitant to identify myself as a conservative. We conserve those things that have proven themselves over time. To bargain away what works for what might work is not a good idea. It is when what is said to work no longer works, that we look for better ways to accomplish the same goal. There is no problem with risking a failed procedure with a new one that holds promise. But to role the dice on life is no sign of intelligence or bravery. The question is, does our economic, social, and political system need a fundamental change? A comparison with other systems around the world will lead the mature intellect to reject such a alternative. Does the existing system need tweaking? To be sure. "Fix it," not "Exchange it," should be our response.

The indirect path to contentment

THERE'S AN OLD SAYING that "a contented man is the one who enjoys the scenery along the detours." Hard to deny the truth of that. We've all been on detours and it's irksome because it prevents us from getting where we want to be when we want to be there. You hear the real problem, don't you? Detours keep *us* from being where *we* want to be when *we* want to be there. Self-concern is the restless expectation that everything work out according to our plans. Our view is that a quality life requires everything to conform to what we want. Little wonder that contentment along the detours of life is a rare quality.

A lot has been written about the subject. *Socrates*, the classical Greek philosopher, taught that the truly rich are those who are content with the least. *Benjamin Franklin* would agree, holding that contentment makes poor men rich. The Hindu swami, *Sivananda*, reasoned that since there is no end to craving, contentment alone is the best way to happiness. Obviously, contentment is a desirable goal. The question comes, how does one achieve it?

I rather think that most people do not consciously organize their life in order to be content. Contentment is expected as a by-product — the by-product of having achieved some other goal. For example, we think that if a person wants to be rich and in fact life turns out that way, then contentment will follow quite naturally. But a careful look at life doesn't support that idea. Too often a person makes it to the top rung of his chosen ladder, only to find it's leaning on the wrong building. Apparently contentment is not the automatic result of achieving some other goal.

I would hold that contentment is the result of intentionally accepting whatever limits life has placed on you. It is not desiring what was never meant to be. Our little Bichon Frise is content

The indirect path to contentment

when her two providers are together. When I drive into the garage, Nelly races to Rachel to announce my arrival. Then its back to me to be sure I haven't wandered off. Once she's brought us together, she goes into a series of uncontrollable wiggles and returns to her favorite place to enjoy the contentment of a job well done. What's her secret for contentment? Realistic expectations and a desire for the common good.

And how does that translate into the busy life of today's young competitor? It suggests that far too much of what we think beneficial is a trap laid by our own egocentricity and that it may well be time to reflect on what is of genuine importance. Contentment is not the fulfillment of personal wants but the laid-back result of embracing life as it is. So when life puts us on a detour, let's allow curiosity to take over and teach us how to enjoy the landscape. The road through life is a one-way trip, so enjoy the scenery as you travel along.

32

The highest form of ignorance

MARK TWAIN THE MOTIVATIONAL speaker and author of more than thirty self-help books, has a number of good insights to share but none better than his observation that, "The highest form of ignorance is when you reject something you don't know anything about." Why this struck me so forcibly is that I have just been reading an account of the life and accomplishments of Francis Collins, the noted physician-geneticist who served as director of the National Human Genome Research Institute. Not only his education background (PhD from Yale and MD from UNC), but his professional achievements in modem molecular genetics cause us to listen when he speaks.

When Dr. Collins was in graduate school he considered himself an atheist, but somewhat later he rather suddenly realized that he had rejected the Christian faith without ever having examined it, and that was diametrically opposed to the scientific method that had ruled his life. It was time to examine his religious view of life, which he did with the help of C S Lewis' *Mere Christianity*. The result was a clear-cut conversion to Evangelical Christianity. What is so interesting to me is that the scientific method, which withholds any conclusion until all the evidence is examined, led a serious and informed intellectual to personal faith in Christ.

It would appear that we are not faced with two kinds of truth: scientific truth which informs us of the universe in which we live, and religious truth that deals with value and other issues that lie beyond our ability to verify. The Christian worldview holds that there is only one kind of truth — what is true in science will not contradict revelation, and what is true in Scripture will not have to be set aside due to the advance of science. Since truth is one, it is perfectly reasonable to expect that everything we know to be true will exhibit an inner consistency. Otherwise truth is something less than we have always understood it to be.

So when we are tempted to reject an area of knowledge of which we are uninformed, we should consider with care the possibility that we may be exhibiting "the highest form of ignorance." This is especially true of the Christian faith because since the dawn of history the spiritual world has played a central role in man's understanding. To ignore it or decide against it apart from careful examination could have some serious and eternal consequences.

How do you feel?

MAYA ANGELOU OBSERVED THAT people will forget what you said and what you did, but not "how you made them feel." Well, it's certainly true that no matter how brilliantly you said it, people will forget it. And in time, what you've done will be forgotten. So the implied dictum is that instead of "saying" and "doing," one should concentrate on making others feel good.

We all know certain people who inevitably leave us feeling good. I still remember a colleague of the '50s who had that knack. Even now I can relive that moment in the coffee shop when, after a guest artist in chapel sang, "His Eye is on the Sparrow," and illustrated it with an octave long glissando, remarked, "I'm sure glad that bird made it down safely."

While I don't disagree with Ms. Angelou regarding the social benefit of making others feel good, I would want to add that it is hardly an ultimate goal in life. Passengers on the Titanic probably enjoyed the first part of the trip, but before long safety became more important. Ultimately, lasting pleasure comes from doing the right thing in the right way. Each of us has an inborn sense of oughtness. We distinguish between what should be and what shouldn't. This may differ somewhat between cultures but the name we give to the person without a moral compass is "psychopath." I would hold that while it is pleasant to make people feel good, it is vital to live in concert with what we know to be right or wrong.

Keep it simple!

JEAN FRANCOIS DE LA Harpe, the French playwright, was of the opinion that "we always weaken whatever we exaggerate." That he was a satirist and often at odds with his literary colleagues gave me pause, but as I thought about what he said, it began to make sense.

Take a good story, for instance. The more it's told the more elaborate it becomes. The higher the fence you had to climb to escape the larger and more ferocious dog (or was it a wolf, whose teeth marks on your leg have now become deep gashes way down to the bone) the less believable and hence less effective the story. People seem to know when a danger becomes so vivid that it didn't really happen that way or a funny situation becomes so hilarious that what actually was doesn't matter.

Exaggeration weakens. To talk and act as though we were more intelligent, successful, classy, than we are, diminishes who we really are in the eyes of others. They say that a work of art is at its best when there remains nothing that can be removed. Extra baggage dulls impact.

So why do we exaggerate? Probably because we believe the opposite. We think telling it with more color will enhance the portrait. Unfortunately the long-awaited picture turns out to be rather a bit drab. Lesson? Authenticity has its own awards. Tell it like it is. Be what you are.

Good old days

QUITE OFTEN YOU HEAR people talking about "the good old days." Were they ever as good we think they were? That's the question. Or does it really make any difference as long as we think they were? Do people keep emailing you those little tests that are supposed to show you how far along the aging process you are? Categories include, "Still walking?" "Your teeth?" "Ready for hospice?" and "Bought your plot yet?" I'm usually well beyond 10 on a score of 1 to 10.

Here are some of the things I remember from the "good old days." Five-cent hamburgers were okay but if you wanted a really good one you had to go to Dave's and pay 10 cents. Lots of meat. I bought my first car (1914 Dodge roadster) along with three other guys for $20. Not a powerful engine so when we went out into the country (away from roads) and found a steep hill we had to go up backward. Gas was about 11 cents a gallon; once during a "gas war" I bought it for 9. You pumped your own gas, and I don't mean you simply got out of your car and put the hose in the tank. Gas was in a tall pump and dispensed by gravity. After dispensing the proper amount, you took hold of the lever and "pumped" the container full again.

We've just passed Thanksgiving on our way to Christmas and have witnessed the spectacle of Black Friday. Two days ahead of time people are camping outside waiting for that magical moment when the doors to postmodernism's paradise are thrown open and the herd stampedes into the facility. I grew up during the Great Depression and we always waited until Christmas Eve to buy anything so we could get it at half price. One year we bought a crokinole board and played it every night until our fingers got so sore we couldn't snap the rings any more.

Clothes were hung on a line to dry. Boys wore Black Bear overalls. Home entertainment was a radio. I was a fan of "Jack Armstrong, the all-American boy" — came on at 5:45. Once a week we watched "The Shadow." Remember the line, "Who knows what evil lurks in the heart of man? The Shadow knows!" In high school I played quarterback on offense and safety on defense. I pole-vaulted in a state meet using a bamboo pole. Learned to drive on the farm and got my first driver's license at 12. One summer my dad couldn't drive west with us (ND to OR) so my brother, at 14, drove Mom, me, and a neighbor lady all the way to Scholls Ferry, OR, 1270 miles (part way the road was upgraded to gravel!)

So those were the good old days? Yes, for me. I lived in a stable home and was taught right from wrong; couldn't understand why anyone wouldn't want to live in North Dakota. Genuinely contented. Don't know how many young people can say that today.

Treasure that lasts

I'VE GOT GREAT NEWS for the thousands who right now are camped outside the Walmarts of America waiting for the doors of Black Friday to open. It's an old American proverb (given musical expression in the 1992 movie, "Mo' Money"), "The best things in life are free." If you're over thirty you recall the tune right now. I submit that the mad rush on the day after Thanksgiving for "stuff" that's not really needed is a poor substitute for all the good things in life that are absolutely free. How many bruises, black eyes, twisted arms and fractured ribs will result from tomorrow's stampede for the unnecessary?

So now you have it. There it is. Sort of a personal reward for swiftness in action, cunning in slipping into the line and sheer bravado in claiming you had in your grip first. But will it satisfy your deeper needs? Now why did you bring that up? I have a right to it. So you do, we all have a right to buy whatever we might want. But was it worth it? Took a half hour to get to the store, another forty-five minutes to find a parking space, a ten-minute walk to the store, half hour to get through the door and three hours to make the purchase. Probably could have bought it next week at near the same price, or within a dollar or so.

Now what was it that the proverb said, "The best things in life are free." They don't cost anything. We could quickly draw up a list, such as each beat of our heart, every breath we breathe, the amazing eye, songbirds and sunsets — but the first that comes to my mind is friendship. Just finished writing a dozen or so letters to friends, some of whom go back over fifty years. Met Bob in a registration line in 1947, Ron at theological seminary in 1952, Beecher at church in 1953, Dick at WKU in 1967, and Eddie, a different Dick and Gary more recently, about 1993. Wonderful guys!

We've worked together, played together, watched our family grow, celebrated life, and more recently touched base with phone calls and get-togethers. No one paid anything for the relationship, apart from genuine concern for the other and integrity in the bond.

How much more satisfying it is to relax and enjoy all the free things of life than to chase after the unattainable, that is, having. No chain saw ever hugged a man or a quilt a woman. Things don't have that ability. We can bestow upon them an odd sort of affection but that's it, no response. The Christian faith teaches that we were made for relationships. The fact that God is a triune being proves that. Of all my relationships, rewarding as they are, nothing quite matches knowing God in a personal way. He made it possible. In another thirty days we will enjoy Christmas, which celebrates the incarnation, the gift of God's son Christ Jesus through whose death and resurrection that fellowship is made possible. And imagine this, it's free! Truly, the best things in life — this life and the one to come — are free!"

How to handle perplexity

AT NINETY-ONE, A PERSON is apt to find himself reflecting on how it might have been had life taken him down a different path. The engineer who plays a bit on the piano might see himself on stage as a renown artist; the successful CEO might question whether "success" was worth it; the academician might ask himself (at least I do) what it would have been like to have been a specialist in generalities rather than a master of the inconsequential. A scientist friend once told me that science was essentially the bringing of order out of chaos. One begins with a great mass of data and seeks a "law" which will bring reasonable clarity. Once that is achieved, science moves to the next level of uncertainty, once again looking for that which will allow yet another step into the unknown.

Isn't that also what a good quotation achieves? When *H G Wells* concluded, "Human history becomes more and more a race between education and catastrophe," wasn't he trying to explain the complexity of life by means of a simple axiom? This new "law" then allows us to move ahead in our understanding of reality. The inherent problem in moving from the world of the verifiable (science) into the world of values (life) makes quotations about life somewhat less reliable. I guess that is why the task of understanding life via reasonable maxims is generally frowned upon by specialists in the humanities. I would like to challenge that reluctance and make a case for "scientific" generalities regarding life.

Is your goal achievable?

"Everybody talks about priorities and very few do anything about it." Who said that? The answer is — I said it. It is simply an observation on life as I have watched it being lived out now for over ninety years. Huge gap between profession and what actually happens in life.

Now that's a rather dreary way to begin. What I had in mind when I sat down was to share what several well-known individuals have identified as the most important thing in their life.

John Wayne said it was "tomorrow."

Audrey Hepburn wanted "to be happy"

The *Dalai Lama* desired "harmony"

Maya Angelou said "courage"

For *John Kennedy* it was "physical fitness"

For *Tim Tebow*, his "relationship with Jesus Christ."

Not a bad collection of goals (I didn't include *Oscar Wilde's* "money" because without a context you might not catch the irony.) Some of them achievable, others less so. However, the question has to arise, "Why do people so regularly fall short of their aspirations?" How often is a New Year's resolution kept? Is it due to some basic flaw in human nature or are the goals too high.

The first suggestion reflects the historic view of the Christian faith that while man was created to mirror the nature of God (we are "his image"), sin entered the picture at the inception of history and crippled man morally so that his essential concern is for self rather than for God and others. And I believe that to be true because it is so clearly taught in Scripture.

However, that is not the entire story. It is also true that people regularly fall short because the moral expectations of Scripture are incredibly high. Let's look at a couple from Jesus' Sermon on the Mount. We will inherit the world if we are "meek," be blessed if we "hunger and thirst for righteousness," and see God if we are "pure in heart" (Matt. 5:5-8). How are we doing on those basic requirements? Has anyone mastered meekness? Do we hunger and thirst for righteousness? And what about purity of heart?

The honest people I know acknowledge defeat. But then what? Does that mean we won't make it? "Well, Jesus didn't mean what he said," is one answer, but it's unacceptable. Jesus either tells the truth or he doesn't. One group within the Christian faith says that that level of living is intended for some future period of time. An older school of thought holds that Jesus' goals are intended to be unreachable — you do your best and when you fail you have to throw yourself on God's mercy, that's what he wanted in the first place.

I believe there is a better answer. The ethical goals of Christianity are not intended to be reached in some quantitative way but serve as guides in the direction that God desires for our lives. To be sincerely headed toward the kind of life that pleases God is to have achieved it. As a parent you wouldn't punish a son who was doing everything he could at his current stage in life to become all that you would like him to be. Only a radical legalist would require perfection in a process toward that which is impossible given our human nature.

Do I have a right to what is yours?

BORN IN NORTH CAROLINA, the fifth child of a housemaid, brought up in Harlem without a father, high school dropout, *Thomas Sowell* had every reason not to succeed. So how is it that a young black like that managed to graduate from three of America's most intellectually elite universities, Harvard, Columbia, and the University of Chicago (PhD) and then go on to teach at several top universities? Currently Dr. Sowell serves as Senior Fellow on Public Policy at Stanford University?

But it is not his achievements in academia that impress me at the moment but his insights into life in today's world. For instance:

"I have never understood why it is greed for a person to keep what he has earned, but not greed to want what someone else has earned."

"What is one person's 'fair share' of what someone else has earned?"

As our struggling and nearly bankrupt nation searches for ways to balance a budget that clearly spends far more than its expected revenue, there has been a lot of talk about morality in a free market system. To what extent are those who do well responsible for those who do not? Is it right for a government to take from one sector and give to another? What is a "fair share?"

I have little expertise on the subject but it seems to me that moral obligation is an individual matter. From a Christian standpoint, if my neighbor is hungry I have the responsibility to share with him what I have. That is something I do as an individual. I do it because it is an expression of brotherly love and that is a moral requirement of the Christian faith. Now, if a dozen families should organize themselves into some sort of social unit, would they as a group (though their leader) be responsible to tell each family how much they should give to the disadvantaged member? Would it be right for the group to tell member A (who has been out of work for six months) to give only a single sack of potatoes, and member B (who happens to have had an exceptionally rewarding year) a truck load of produce? I think not. Supplying the need of another is the responsibility of the individual. To shift it away from the individual to some sort of group effort is to deprive the individual of the personal pleasure of meeting the need of another. That runs contrary to what is best both for the individual and for society at large.

To answer the earlier question, I would say that no one has a "right" to what belongs to another, and that ultimately the question of "fair share" is something that each person must work out with God.

Do habits help?

DOSTOEVSKY'S OBSERVATION THAT "THE second half of a man's life is made up of nothing but the habits he has acquired during the first half" set me to thinking about the way we go about living. By and large, most everything we do is an expression of a habit. Many of us sleep in on Saturday because we've always slept in on Saturday. We have an early cup of coffee and get ready to watch a game (doesn't everybody?). We are truly creatures of habit. It is a comfortable way to live and involves little or no conscious thought.

But are habits good? In what way do they aid us in our progress toward life's goal? Why is it that good habits have to be formed but we simply fall into bad habits? A lot of questions can be raised on the subject.

Obviously, some habits are good, they help us get where we want to be. If physical wellbeing is a goal, then regular exercise and a proper diet are habits that help us get there. If we have always gone to the gym three times a week then we don't have to ponder the question when the time arrives. Habit is a faithful friend who helps us toward our goal. But it is equally true that some habits work against our best interests. In fact, they are unusually powerful in denying us our goals. As the old saying goes, "Habits are like a comfortable bed, easy to get into but hard to get out of."

It has often been observed that character is the sum total of our habits. The sequence runs like this: what we think we say; what we say we do; what we do becomes habit, which shapes character and determines destiny. To the extent this is true, and I believe it is, habit is perhaps the crucial element in the formation of character. Good habits are powerful agents toward a desirable end but bad habits are equally powerful in preventing it.

This being true, the role of "what we always do" requires our attention. What is it that I always do that helps and what do I always do that hinders? If I can determine that, I can readjust my life toward the more desirable goals. And the sooner I do it the better, because, as the Chinese proverb has it, "Habits are cobwebs at first; cables at last." To develop a profitable habit, one must genuinely want to. Desires unable to move us to action are useless at best. Effective desire does what is required to realize its aspirations. So the question is up to the individual, do I care enough about what I want to establish a pattern that will take me there? If not, forget it.

It is interesting that habit makes the task easier. Rather than being an endless responsibility to do the right thing, it becomes a way of living that provides its own motivation. So here's to custom in life! One might even call it conservatism. But let's be careful that the things we do by habit are taking us where we want to go.

Why are you happy?

WHEN I READ ERNEST Hemingway's conjecture that "Happiness in intelligent people is the rarest thing I know," my immediate reaction was to scan my own group of friends. It didn't seem to pan out. Over the years I have gathered (somewhat automatically) a circle of friends that includes relatively well-known leaders in various segments of society as well as a Guatemalan peasant unknown outside of his own family. I did not find a scale of happiness rising from some degree of misery for the wealthy to a higher degree of contentment for those who possessed less. However, neither did I find the opposite.

In the process, I had to ask myself the obvious question, what is happiness? Obviously it is important because along with life and liberty, the Declaration of Independence tells us that the pursuit of happiness is an inalienable right. At that point I decided to check with the authorities only to discover that the subject has been under discussion for as far back as we have written records. Some 300 years BC the Confucian thinker Mencius taught that joy in life comes as a result of practicing the great virtues. In Buddhism, ultimate happiness is the reward of overcoming craving. In the thirteenth century Thomas Aquinas, the Italian philosopher and theologian, taught that happiness was the result of contemplating the divine which would then inform the intellect as it directed one's life.

More recently, Sonja Lyubomirsky, a professor in psychology at UC Riverside, has concluded that 50% of happiness is genetically determined, 10% relates to the circumstances of life, and 40% is subject to self-control. If this is true, and I believe it is, it suggests that we have a very good chance for happiness by simply choosing it and taking appropriate steps. But this seems to run contrary to

Hemingway's observation that happiness is a rare trait among intelligent people. Could it be that "intelligent" and "wise" are not the same? It may be that for the average person the former term means something like having a detailed knowledge of an area and the latter as expressing how that knowledge may be applied to life. This would explain why Hemingway's "intelligent" people are not necessarily happy and why a "wise" person is far more apt to be happy.

While happiness may be difficult to define, it is not difficult to recognize when it happens. And in a broad sense, everyone knows what it means to be happy and it doesn't make a lot of difference whether it is defined hedonistically as the result of seeking pleasant experiences and avoiding the unpleasant, or in the classic Greek sense (the eudaimonic tradition) as the result of living life in a full and deeply satisfying way. As once again I scan my own friends, the accumulation of wealth has little or nothing to do with the degree of their happiness. For me, and those I'm pleased to name as friends, happiness has come as a result of knowing God in a personal way through the redemptive work of Christ on the cross. On a practical level the pleasure of each day is, to a significant extent, determined by how this relationship to God is allowed to control both our thoughts and our actions.

Why call a judge "The Honorable So and So?"

WHAT ARE WE SAYING when we refer to a judge as "the Honorable So and So? The very title "Honorable" expresses our recognition that we live in a moral world where the concept of right and wrong is accepted. One dictionary defines honor as "strict conformity to what is considered morally right."

But where do moral systems come from? Was it custom that decided that one thing is right and another wrong? Is theft wrong simply because it has always been considered wrong? If social practice determined morality, we'd be living in a world where the essential questions of morality were accidental. In some social groups stealing could be right and in others wrong because that's the way it had always been.

Somehow this is not a satisfactory answer. I believe the vast majority of people would agree that moral responsibility requires something beyond custom, some outside force, some absolute. One thing is for sure and that is that our sense of "oughtness" didn't create itself. The Christian faith holds that God is the source of our responsibility to do what is right and not do what is wrong. So, for the Christian to live an honorable life requires that they conform to what God has declared morally right. Anything else is dishonorable.

The theological expression, the righteousness of God, is often thought of in a sort of abstract way but the truth is that it is a description of the One who always does what is right. A judge is given the title "Honorable" because it is his responsibility to decide if a given act is right or wrong. God is honorable because it is his very nature. His requirements are an expression of who he is.

It is interesting that this basic Judeo-Christian precept finds expression in the Greek classical period. *Socrates* said, "The greatest way to live with honor in this world is to be what we pretend to be." Honor is the correlation between what a person says and does. To live in an honorable way is essentially to be in life, what we claim to be. It's the old "walk-the-talk" challenge. As always, contemporary public life continues to demonstrate that, whatever the problem, it is someone else's fault. What a dramatic change if those in power would accept the responsibility for what they do. To be honorable one must act in honorable ways. The universal tendency to pretend we are someone different than we really are (the one who didn't do it, say it, think it, is responsible for it) is dishonorable and ought to be designated as such. Transparency is widely recognized as a virtue in our system of governance, but if it exists in theory only it is worthless, and, in fact, dishonorable.

How pygmies become giants

Isaac Asimov, professor of biochemistry and prolific author of science fiction, concluded that, "The saddest aspect of life right now is that science gathers knowledge faster than society gathers wisdom." And who can deny the rapidity with which technology is changing the face of contemporary life. Not long ago I attended a church where the rather flamboyant young minister excitedly delivered his sermon with the help of an electronic tablet carefully disguised as a leather-bound Bible. My fear during the entire sermon was that the text might strangely disappear and the minister would have to pause and reboot. I don't know, but perhaps there already are churches in America where you can download the sermon, make your donation by electronic transfer, and fellowship with other members via Facebook. I can see it now, plastered across the stained-glass window — "No tweeting during the sermon!" Tom Lantos (of the House Foreign Affairs Committee) was absolutely right when he characterized his opposition as "technological giants" yet, unfortunately, "moral pygmies." There may not be a cause and effect relationship, but advance in one area seems to be accompanied by a decline in the other.

Why is it that the mind of man embraces the unknown and can hardly wait to take on the next intellectual challenge, while the heart of man seems to resist every attempt to redirect it away from moral improvement? It is exciting to learn what technology has in store for us, but boring to think about how we could conduct our lives better. What will be trumps what should be? Why is that? For me, the answer seems to be rather clear. But then, I've chosen to approach all of life from a biblical point of view and that clarifies issues. My basic presupposition is that God exists. The materialistic approach narrows reality to what can be verified by the limited methods of science. The idea that nothing exists outside the material is itself an assumption, not provable by definition. So I am not in the least embarrassed by any supposed inferiority of matters that lie outside the realm of what science can verify.

So, the widely accepted observation that man, morally speaking, is more a pygmy than a giant is consistent with the biblical teaching of his nature. Made in the image of God but victimized by a decision to go his own way explains why technological advance is not necessarily accompanied by ethical growth. The former deals with the mind and the latter with the heart. For man to survive does not depend on his intellectual brilliance but upon his willingness to do the right thing. What is required is a renewal of the heart and this calls for the supernatural work of God. Scripture uses a very simple term to describe this remarkable change — it is a "new birth." The only answer for the universal rush toward annihilation is moral regeneration. That alone is God's answer for the giant-pigmy problem.

Avoiding the unavoidable

H. G. WELLS WAS quite certain that "human history becomes more and more a race between education and catastrophe." It appears from this that he understood man's basic problem to be intellectual. It only we would learn to think correctly then we could escape global disaster. Simply put, think right and you will do right.

What troubles me with this scenario is what happened in Germany leading up to the Third Reich. There are few if any nations that can boast a higher level of intellectual accomplishment. German universities were among the very best. Prizes in science, the arts, and humanities were regularly rewarded to outstanding individuals and institutions. However intellectual achievement did not prevent plans for the total eradication of some 11 million Jewish people. It would appear that the moral flaw in man cannot be healed by more education.

The Judeo-Christian understanding of the nature of man provides a far better understanding of society's moral decline. It holds that man is created in the image of God but has fallen. God created us in such a way that we could sustain a personal relationship with him but that involved free choice. In our freedom to disobey we chose to separate ourselves from the creator. Theology refers to that fateful decision as the fall of man. Our understanding, our will, and our emotions have become distorted by our willful separation from God. We do not think correctly, make the right choices, nor relate adequately to God.

I certainly agree with Wells as to an approaching catastrophe, but disagree rather emphatically that something short of moral realignment can answer our problem. The problem is man's heart, not his mind. Once again, the Christian faith has the only adequate answer. Sine we are unable to help ourselves, God sent his Son as a sacrifice for our sinful departure from that prior relationship. By faith we are enabled to accept the gift and become what he always intended us to be. As man turns to God, personal calamity is avoided. By a major turning to God by increasing numbers, the calamity envisioned by Wells could be avoided.

The magic of music

As far back as we can remember people having been doing their best to explain what music really is. Music has been defined as "the strongest form of magic," "the speech of angels," "love looking for words," but perhaps it is best understood in terms of what it does. *Sir Thomas Beecham,* director of the Royal Philharmonic orchestra, was directly on target when he said, "The function of music is to release us from the tyranny of conscious thought." As I understand it, he is saying that music provides the escape route from the banal to the beautiful, from thinking about what is necessary to experiencing what is beyond.

And it's true — music creates a relationship deeper by far than any amount of chitchat. It lifts us out of the ordinary and allows us to experience reality on a distinctly higher level. It is interesting that just as I was about to post this blog I heard Andre Rieu and his group perform a stirring rendition of "You'll Never Walk Alone." The camera showed men and women in tears throughout the audience of several thousand. Powerful music causes us to relive the moving periods of personal history. Before I began to teach at the university level I was a student somewhere (grade school to postdoc) for more than two-dozen years. But a simple song in the right setting provides a greater aesthetic experience than years of rearranging footnotes.

I am not suggesting that learning is a necessary and dull part of living. Anything but! The excitement of suddenly seeing how two disparate ideas can relate so as to significantly advance our understanding is considerable. The pleasure of an intellectual discovery normally follows a great deal of careful thought. Music, however, yields its charms to those who relax and let it perform its magic.

Music may not always place us in some exalted sphere, but it does demand control. The heavy beat of passion won't allow us to be indifferent. The siren sweet melody of nostalgia cannot be ignored. Good music takes control. It sets us free from a world that denies the existence of anything that can't be verbalized. Sir Henry calls it "the tyranny of conscious thought." The human experience is more than thinking and doing. It is also feeling, in the more profound sense. A life devoid of moments of ecstatic response to the best in music falls short of what it means to be alive.

Why we are like we are

FROM TIME TO TIME I have said that my purpose in this blog is to reflect upon various quotations that have piqued my curiosity and do it from a Christian world-view. At this point it may be helpful to say something about that term since it originated in another culture. World-view is the English equivalent of the German *Weltanschauung* (from *Welt*, world, and *Anschauung*, perception). The World English Dictionary defines *Weltanschauung* as "a comprehensive view or personal philosophy of human life and the universe." It is a way of looking at the totality of human existence here on planet earth. It is our perception of reality.

When I say Christian world-view I am asserting that the Christian faith, based upon God's self-revelation in Scripture, has a specific way of looking at what is. For example, it holds that God created the world and thus differs from the philosophical materialist who claims no knowledge of how matter came about but is sure that nothing else exists. This is not an insignificant difference. The fact that a supernatural being exists carries the strong possibility that life here on earth brings with it some sense of obligation. If, on the other hand, what is, is simply a normal development in the material realm, then it would be hard to understand why I ought to do this instead of that. The Christian world-view holds very distinctly that man's obligation is to conform to the expectations of his Creator. A world-view that posits God wants to live in a way that will please him. If there is no God, there is no one to please.

One of the areas that exhibit the superiority of the Christian world-view is social responsibility. Fifty some years ago President Johnson launched the war on poverty. Over $16 trillion has been spent and the percentage living in poverty now is roughly the same. Why is that? The Christian world-view proposes care for the widow and orphan (James 1:27) but also says, "The one who is unwilling to work shall not eat" (2 Thess. 3:10). If everyone would take that seriously, the situation would change dramatically.

Another area where world-view makes a difference is the nature of man. Nothing explains the conflicting qualities of ego-centricity and nobility as well as the Biblical teaching that man is made in the image of God (has certain qualities that reflect the nature of God) yet by a sinful choice to go it on his own (the fall in Eden) has allowed sin to control his actions. He will dive into the raging stream to save a child yet live out his days in selfish concern for what is best for him.

World-views are not provable. They lie outside reason's domain. But there are ways to satisfy the responsible person that some ways of thinking about life are better than others. The theologian/philosopher John Edward Carnell used to say that one set of presuppositions is preferable to another if (1) they are inwardly consistent, and (2) they answer better to life as one experiences it. On that a basis, I am confident that the Biblical approach to understanding mankind (specifically, why we do what we do) is far superior to all competing views.

The playful nature of humor

I KEEP WONDERING WHY certain things strike me as funny. Why is it that I can't help but smile when I read *Groucho Marx's* response to a recently published acquaintance, "From the moment I picked your book up until I laid it down I was convulsed with laughter. Some day I intend reading it." Why does a joke like that make the day a bit more fun? What is humor? I recognize it when I hear it, but what is it?

So I made the mistake of looking up "humor" in the dictionary and, among the several drab definitions, I found it was "the faculty of expressing the amusing." So I went to the Internet and asked "Ask.com" only to find that "humor is something that makes us laugh." Yes, but what is it?

Okay, let's just think about it. The first thing that strikes me about a joke is that it seems always to have an element of incongruity about it. For example, since there is no number 11 on the phone, the blonde couldn't call emergency. Or, if at first you don't succeed, skydiving is not for you. Humor walks around the corner and suddenly bumps into something you'd never expect to be there. A talking dog, a golfer who comes closer to the ball every time he swings, a skeleton who needs some body to dance with.

Incongruity is by definition absurd. Our minds apparently take pleasure in being tricked. Since most of our thinking is relatively straight forward, any sudden absurdity strikes us as comical. We laugh when a nattily dressed man slips and falls on the dance floor. We've probably seen it too many times but the old pie-in-the-face still brings a smile. On a somewhat higher level, wit is a form of humor that appeals to the quick and clever mind. Charles Brooks describes wit as "a lean creature with a sharp inquiring nose, whereas humor has a kindly eye and a comfortable girth."

So a joke is good if it presents some juxtaposition of opposites that suddenly presents the mind with a totally unexpected relationship. Groucho says that he picked up the book and was convulsed with laughter. We thought, of course, that he had read it; not so. He laughed AT the book, not because of it. Some day he may read it.

Know any good jokes?

Are you the person I'm talking to?

SOCRATES ONCE OBSERVED, "THE greatest way to live with honor in this world is to be what we pretend to be." I have never heard of a nation or tribal culture that prizes hypocrisy. It seems as though everyone everywhere wants other people to be what they claim to be. It's interesting that the only group of people criticized by Jesus were the hypocrites. He didn't condemn the woman caught in adultery but simply said, "Don't sin anymore" (John 8:11). He ate and drank with common people until some considered him a glutton and a drunkard (Luke 7:34). But seven times in one chapter of the Gospel of Matthew, Jesus condemns the religious authorities, calling them "hypocrites" (chapter 23).

In ancient Greece a *hypokrites* was a person who acted on the stage, pretended, often wore a mask. He wanted to do two things at once: hide his true identity, and appear to be some one other than himself. It is understandable that everyone would like to hide certain negative traits. As we well know, "No one is perfect." We are not quite so willing, however, to admit that we often go out of our way to make the other person believe that we are more kind, thoughtful, intelligent, honest, whatever, than we are. The opinions of others seem to matter so we adjust to expectations and act out the part. It's called hypocrisy.

One advantage of realizing a natural tendency is that we can take steps that turn life in a more positive direction. Socrates said it was honorable to do our best "to be what we pretend to be." If we pretend to be more cordial than we really are, it would be a good idea to consider the social benefits of cordiality and look for opportunities to be genuinely cordial. We may find ourselves actually becoming what we pretend to be. Very few people pretend to be worse than they are so it's a win-win situation. Insight into our tendency to make ourselves appear to be better than we are could in the long run produce a better society. I'm not ready to shout, "Long live hypocrisy," but I do hold that we have the ability to turn a negative into a positive. But do we have the will? Well, that's a decision for each of us.

Why are you less important than me?

LAST EVENING ON "SHARK Tank" *Mark Cuban*, owner of the Dallas Mavericks, came up with a bit of advice that struck me as right on target. He said, "Never take advice from anyone who doesn't have to live with the consequences." Granted, it probably will never go down in history as one of the fifty best quotes of all time, but before you dismiss it, let's give it a moment.

Advice comes easy. Just "ask and you will receive" (to borrow a biblical phrase). Almost everyone has an answer to any question you might ask. Where is the best place to live? What should I do to stop a run-away horse? Why should I get my news from the Internet? How can I get this thing opened? It is so easy to get advice from those who will not be affected by your decision. And that, precisely, is the problem. There is something about the human specie that enables us to provide quick answers to issues that don't affect us. I know that if I have a cup of rich coffee late in the evening, it will be almost morning by the time I drop off to sleep. So, I give up late evening coffee. However, if you should ask me whether YOU should have a cup at 11 PM, I might say, "It's up to you," or, "Why not!" Why don't I ask you how drinking coffee late in the evening affects you? The answer is that by nature we are hopelessly egocentric. We came into the world that way and progress is either slow or nonexistent. Christian theology calls it "the fall." God made us in his image — that is, that we might sustain a relationship to him. But when the primal pair decided against God's restriction and for the "advice" of the Tempter, they transitioned to a condition in which they were doomed to live primarily, if not absolutely, for themselves.

Is there a remedy? Christian theology says Yes. The gift of God's Son was a sacrifice for our sin (i.e., our egocentricity) to be received by faith so that our initial relationship might be restored. Unfortunately that process is incredibly slow. As we are gradually released from what we became by deciding to go it on our own, we are empowered by the Spirit to do such things as to remind our questioner of possible consequences.

The corrupting influence of power

Lin Yutang, the influential Chinese writer, noted that "when small men begin to cast big shadows, it means that the sun is about to set." We know that great men cast big shadows and nations are blessed by the impact of their lives and the legacies they leave. But there are also small men who cast big shadows and society is left in shambles. History has a way of producing its fair share of Hitlers, Stalins, Pol Pots, and Kim Jong-ils and they all cast enormous shadows. As the sun goes down, millions are adversely affected by their reigns.

There is no question but there are plenty of big men in this world — good men who are living out their days in a fair and honorable way. They pay their taxes, get along with their neighbors, work hard, raise good kids, contribute to charity, etc. Then why do "small men" seem so often to be in charge? What is there about power that attracts? Christian theology teaches that man (and I uses the word genetically) is a creature made in God's image but flawed by disobedience. The result is universal narcissism. Power is the political aphrodisiac that all too often draws the unqualified into public office. Plato was right when he said, "One of the penalties for refusing to participate in politics is that you end up being governed by your inferiors." What a nation needs in positions of leadership are good men able to resist the corrupting influence of power.

Is God a comedian?

WHAT DID *VOLTAIRE* MEAN when he said, "God is a comedian playing to an audience too afraid to laugh"? This renowned French writer and polemicist of the Enlightenment was known for his wit, so did he intend us to take this remark somewhat whimsically or not? Let's see what we can make of it.

Voltaire was a deist. Believing in God was not a matter of faith but of reason. It was perfectly evident to him that there existed a necessary, eternal, Supreme Being. So in what sense was God a "comedian?" Perhaps because he created man. Or beyond that, the animal world (there are some strange looking creatures out there.) But let's stick with man. Man is a strange being. I'm sure that as Voltaire observed the customs of his day, the tendency of his fellow citizens to bungle the affairs of life, the self-destructive nature of human conduct, he must have thought either that God had made a mistake of tragic proportions or that it was for his own amusement.

But what about man being "too afraid to laugh?" It is true that those who understand at some depths the current state of world affairs are not comfortable about the future. The dominoes of the last stage of history are all lined up and the first is ready to topple. The only thing that could be "funny" about that is that man would be responsible for his own demise.

My trouble with all this is that it makes God less than good. I can see God as a comedian but not at the expense of his own creation. That's not funny. The God revealed In Scripture is a God of supreme love. The gift of his Son as an atonement for man's sin rules out any possibility of him acting otherwise. I certainly have a lot of trouble seeing God as a comedian if we use late night show hosts as the model. But does he have a sense of humor? Of that I am sure because humor adds so much to life and, as John has it (10:10), Jesus came that we might have life "more abundantly."

About man, are we "too afraid to laugh?" I believe that depends upon what segment of the human race we are talking about. I'm quite sure that many are, because they don't do anything about it. Some are fearful, especially when age or disaster brings them face to face with eternity. Those who face the future with glad expectation are those who through faith have come to grips with reality; those whose faith rests securely in the hands of the One who on Easter morning broke the bonds of death and provided the way to eternal joy.

"It's not that simple"

Ever read something from a well-known author that strikes you as simply wrong? That was my reaction to *Oscar Wilde's* comment that "truth is rarely pure and never simple. Modern life would be very tedious if it were either, and modern literature a complete impossibility!" I believe the exact opposite; let me tell you why.

Many years ago a scientist friend shared with me his understanding of how the scientific method works. You begin with a mass of seemingly unrelated data and in time you discover how they are associated and posit a "law" (drop something a thousand times and it always seems to head for the floor — Aha! gravity). Then you move to a slightly higher level of incongruity equipped now with a "law." The same process eventually brings further clarification. You breathe a "now I see" sigh of relief. To put it simply, science is replacing confusion with simplicity. What specifically interested me is that this process is also true in other fields of learning. While the advance in any field brings a new level of confusion, the ultimate result is an informed simplicity. Karl Barth, the most influential theologian since Thomas Aquinas, summarized his massive 4-volume Church Dogatics, saying, "Jesus loves me, this I know, for the Bible tells me so." Truth, for this intellectual giant, was pure and simple.

How many times in a discussion in which you are about to establish your position you hear the caveat, "It's not that simple." The opposition would have you believe that there is a lot more involved in the issue and that you have unwisely chosen to settle for a simplistic answer. No evidence to the contrary is set forth so there is no way to further establish your position. Beyond that, the certainty with which the mantra is spoken suggests that the other person has a vast store of knowledge on the subject which, if brought into the discussion would reveal how uninformed and simplistic your conclusion really is. I would like to suggest that "It's not that simple" is, more often than not, nothing more than a maneuver to gain advantage.

Now I'm not suggesting that all life is so simple that it can be understood without serious reflection. What I am suggesting is that most issues, when studied with care, can be expressed in genuinely simple terms. So often intellectual verbiage is a path away from truth and serves the egocentricity of the discussant rather than a mutual understanding of the issue. For instance, to return to Karl Barth, no one denies our human inability to grasp the "complexity" of a triune God who speaks into existence all that is. But at the same time, few can deny the existential reality of the simple statement, "Jesus loves me, this I know, for the Bible tells me so." In matters eternal we must think with our heart.

Humor, the best medicine

HUMOR MAY THE BEST medicine after all. At least that is what the former editor of the Saturday Review believed. You may remember that following a serious heart attack and being hospitalized at UCLA, *Norman Cousins* decided to contrive his own remedy. He took massive doses of vitamin C and watched the antics of the Marx Brothers. Although he was given little chance of surviving he was with us for ten years following his first heart attack. He found that ten minutes of genuine belly laugh would give him at least two hours of pain-free sleep. This "joyous discovery" led to an adjunct professorship in the university's School of Medicine.

Humor is not only fun but physically helpful as well. And it takes many forms, all the way from shaggy dogs stories that test one's patience to the quick witticism that catches you unawares. Since it is free, why don't we use it more for the aches and pains of body and soul? I think it's because natural disposition heads the other direction. That's not to say that normal life doesn't have its happy moments but simply that it's all too human to be overly serious. We tend to trudge through the day when we'd get there in a better mood if we'd try skipping.

And this takes a decision — the decision that today will be far brighter if I decide that it will. Our approach to the day inevitably determines how the day will be. And my today is going to start with some of the silliness (and remember, the Marx brothers were silly) in which I indulge from time to time. I may have to apologize for it, but I happen to like the antics of *Steve Martin*. His observation that, "First the doctor told me the good news: I was going to have a disease named after me," still brings a smile. *Mark Twain* confessed, "There is nothing so annoying as to have two people go right on talking when you're interrupting." *Al McGuire* wondered why "kamikaze pilots wore helmets" and *Mark Russell* supported the scientific theory that "the rings of Saturn are composed entirely of lost airline luggage." If you haven't stopped reading by now you'll probably identify with the man who confessed that he was "such an ugly kid that when he played in the sandbox the cat kept trying to cover him up."

Have a great week!

The can can't be kicked without a kicker

HOW MANY TIMES IN the past week or so when the federal government has been "shut down" have we heard the trite expression "to kick the can down the road?" I remember as a boy we used to play "kick the can" in a nearby alley but the goal there was to run in from hiding and kick the can so those who had been caught trying to kick it would be released from "jail." In that setting you might say that kicking the can was a brave and noble act because it involved personal risk for the benefit of others. The way the phrase is used now is quite the opposite — it is the evasion of obligation for personal gain. For example, an extremely serious national financial problem affecting the lives of the American people is postponed by our elected representatives in Washington because taking a moral stand on the issue might endanger their reelection.

There is no question that the less important should be postponed (if necessary) so the more important can be realized. We all recognize that. But a nation that has now accumulated over $17,000,000,000,000 in debt should not kick that "can" any further down the road (excuse my use of the tired idiom but it does present the problem rather well.) What is happening here is a serious collapse of morality at a level in society that hurts those who have placed their confidence in their representatives. Whenever personal benefit trumps the welfare of the other the law of love has been violated and national heartache, not health, becomes the destination. The essential ethic of a Judeo-Christian civilization (and the western world is/was one) is love (see Mark 12:29-31). Unnecessary postponement of essential legislature (kicking the can) is a national tragedy.

But isn't it our fault when our representatives fail to live up to their responsibilities? Well, it is certainly our fault if they are reelected to office. That has been common knowledge since *Plato* (Greek philosopher who in the 5th century BC helped lay the foundation for Western civilization) who said that "one of the penalties for refusing to participate in politics is that you end up being governed by your inferiors." Unfortunately when a governing system reaches a certain level of complexity it begins to feed on itself and, like the cancer cell, takes over and ultimately destroys. The answer to the "kick the can" problem in a democracy is to remove the kicker. See you at the polling place.

Leaders make it happen

"TO LEAD THE ORCHESTRA you must turn your back on the crowd" is *James Crooks'* advice for those who would lead in any field. Leading from behind may be a valid principle for management but not for leadership. The effective leader doesn't ask where his constituents want to go, but turns them in the direction they should go. This requires both vision and resilience.

Every field has its leaders. Never do they strike us as average individuals performing at a slightly higher level than their colleagues. They seem to have an uncanny sense of which route will take us where we should go. We may or may not ever get there but along the way we will have a growing respect for the one who could look beyond and have the courage to head us in that direction. Quite a bit has been written on the difference between coercive and authentic leadership. History is full of examples of leaders who by sheer force have taken a nation to an undesirable goal. Who would have thought that a nation like Germany, as advanced and sophisticated as it was in the early 20th century, would have earned a reputation for unimaginable cruelty? Coercive leadership in any of its forms is an admission of moral bankruptcy.

Effective leaders focus on the raison d'être of the organization. Their role is to make it possible for the group to get to where it should go. Discovering new goals is more the task of the visionary. JFK didn't tell us that it would be a good idea to go to the moon (as if no one had ever thought of that before) but redirected our energies so we actually got there. Had he kept looking at the audience he could never have conducted the orchestra. We all had our instruments ready but someone had to give the downbeat. That is the essence of leadership — not to ask the musicians what they would like to play but to give them the score and tell them it is time to start.

A problem only congress can't see

IF YOU DO A computer search on "leadership," Google will give you 138,000,000 references in less than one second. Wow! Apparently we know a lot about leadership. We can define it, discuss it, illustrate it — but have trouble finding real life examples. More often than not it evades us in our search for the "right" leader. We want our leader to be a person of integrity, fully informed on crucial issues, sensitive to the rights of minorities, eloquent in presentation, and aware of the concerns of a diverse society. There is nothing wrong with these qualifications. They take us in the right direction. However, there is an additional quality that is rarely mentioned in a discussion on leadership. The American humorist, *Arnold H. Glasgow* was on target when he wrote, "One of the true tests of leadership is the ability to recognize a problem before it becomes an emergency." This requires the common sense ability to learn from past experience.

We readily acknowledge that "history repeats itself" but have trouble acting accordingly. We know that if a person drives recklessly it's only a matter of time until they'll have an accident. For a leader to be unaware of probable consequences or unwilling to take appropriate action indicates rather obviously that they are the wrong person for the position. On every level, a leader must be able to recognize that it is unwise to pursue a course of action that in the past has led to an undesirable result. Misguided policies should be abandoned. We know that if you bang your head on the table you'll get a headache. In the same way, if a nation weakens its ability to defend itself, others will take advantage. They always have, they always will — cause and effect.

And there are other problems that become emergencies if a nation doesn't take appropriate action. Certainly one is our spending problem. What would you, as the one responsible, do if the family debt were significantly above your income? What would happen in your family if an able-bodied member refused to work? How long would your family allow one of its members pursue a life-style that had proven to be personally harmful as well as detrimental for the others? Such problems are not too hard to understand, are they? We would quit spending so much, make the lazy do something to help, and do our best to assist the wayward in changing their destructive habits.

So why don't we as a nation acknowledge our problems and take the action necessary to solve them? Why is it that we allow an unsustainable debt to continue to grow? We are told that under the current administration, for every job created 45 people have been added to the food stamp roster. No patriot wants to witness the demise of our nation. So where is the leadership that will redirect us away from the inevitable result of our current set of priorities? A wise father doesn't spend more than he earns, teaches his children their obligations as a member of the family, and helps the black sheep turn from their destructive lifestyle and enjoy the proven benefits of a life with boundaries. Is there a leader on the national stage willing and able to direct a profligate people back to those values that made us what we once were?

It's too early to get old

MARY ANNE EVANS (OR *George Eliot* as she was known in her writings) was an English novelist of the Victorian era, known for her realism and psychological insight (novels include such notable works as *Adam Bede,* and *Silas Mariner*). She is quoted as having said, "It is never too late to be what you might have been." I genuinely like that. Having lived three years in a retirement home (and it had everything that a good retirement home should have) I began to realize that its very ambiance was redirecting my focus toward the past. What was becoming important was either what had been or one's health. As one resident said, "Ask a person how he is and you get an organ recital." I don't mean to belittle the aging process but George Eliot's reminder that "It is never to late" is a strong deterrent to what might be called the premature surrender of life. Let's think about it.

Along with taxes, death is inevitable. The oldest person, whose life span can be validated, was Jeanne Calment, a French woman who died in 1995. She lived for 122 years and 164 days. She is quoted as saying, "I've never had but one wrinkle and I'm sitting on it." She may have lost her health but not her sense of humor. Life can be a wonderful sequence of experiences from the innocence of childhood, through the frantic activity of adulthood, to the serenity of age. In so many ways the latter days of life can be the best. We enjoyed the zest of youth, then the challenge of the productive years, and now we have the opportunity to enter a time of reflection on what is truly important. I'm speaking in generalities of course, but what is generally true is not invalidated by the exception — the exception merely "proves [or tests] the rule." Rather than resist aging would it not be better to embrace it?

And how does this relate to becoming what we might have been? It doesn't mean to do what we might have done or to get what we might have had, but to be become what we might have been. Life is about being, not doing or having. If our personal history doesn't sketch a lifetime of authenticity — and that's quite true of everyone — there is still time to live out our days as one could wish they might always have been. The trick is to live each moment true to the way we know it should be — no subterfuge, no duplicity, no pretense, no casuistry. Impossible, you say. I don't think so. At least it deserves the decision to try. For the Christian additional help is provided by the Holy Spirit. It was Jesus who said that "with God all things are possible" (Matt 19:26). The close of life can be better than the beginning because the redirection from doing and having to being is life's most exciting and rewarding experience.

Jesus, deluded or divine?

AT A DINNER IN 1962, honoring American Nobel Prize winners, President *John Kennedy* remarked that that occasion was "the most extraordinary collection of talent, of human knowledge, that has ever been gathered together at the White House, with the possible exception of when Thomas Jefferson dined alone." Few would disagree. Thomas Jefferson, the principal author of our Declaration of Independence and third President of the United States, was a man of extraordinary intellect. Which, for some, raises the question of how a man of such exceptional acumen could separate what he understood as the basic moral code of Jesus from the man himself as presented in the Gospels.

In his work, *The Life and Morals of Jesus of Nazareth* (generally referred to as "The Jefferson Bible") Jefferson, with the aid of a razor, selected and cut from the Bible verses from the four gospels and arranged them chronologically to produce a sort of gospel harmony. In this selective process he gathered what he felt were the essential moral principals taught by Jesus. What he omitted were all the miracles of Jesus and most references to anything that would seem to be supernatural. Passages containing references to the resurrection are missing as well as anything that might suggest that Jesus was divine.

My problem with this is fairly straightforward; can you separate the message (in this case, a part of the message) from the man? The two are inseparably entwined. One of the early scholars to point out the logical impossibility of such a separation was the Scottish "Rabbi" John Duncan who some 150 years ago wrote that "Christ either deceived mankind by conscious fraud, or He was Himself deluded and self-deceived, or He was Divine. There is no getting out of this trilemma. It is inexorable." The miracles that

Jesus performed and his claim of deity make him fraudulent, deluded or divine. There is no other option.

The author most quoted on this is the renown C S Lewis who, in this well-known book, *Mere Christianity*, wrote: "I am trying here to prevent anyone saying the really foolish thing that people often say about Him: I'm ready to accept Jesus as a great moral teacher, but I don't accept his claim to be God. That is the one thing we must not say. A man who was merely a man and said the sort of things Jesus said would not be a great moral teacher. He would either be a lunatic — on the level with the man who says he is a poached egg — or else he would be the Devil of Hell. You must make your choice. Either this man was, and is, the Son of God, or else a madman or something worse. You can shut him up for a fool, you can spit at him and kill him as a demon or you can fall at his feet and call him Lord and God, but let us not come with any patronizing nonsense about his being a great human teacher. He has not left that open to us. He did not intend to. Now it seems to me obvious that He was neither a lunatic nor a fiend: and consequently, however strange or terrifying or unlikely it may seem, I have to accept the view that He was and is God."

At this point I must confess no one could have made the point more convincingly. I admire Jefferson but I agree with Lewis.

Leaving logic, where do we go?

As every schoolchild knows, *Albert Einstein* was a truly remarkable man. In addition to his work in theoretical physics (his theory of relativity is one of the two foundational concepts in modern physics) he had a lot to say about life in general. What I want to question today is his suggestion that "logic will get you from A to B; imagination will take you anywhere."

In order to get started we will have to assume that logic in fact get us from A to B. It seems reasonable, although I rather suspect that one ought to identify both A and B before going on from there. They could exist in distinct domains, in which case there is no logical path that can join them. And logic itself is not incontrovertible proof of reality. As one wag put it, "Logic is an organized way of going wrong." But for the moment let's assume that it is true to say that logical thought takes us in an organized fashion from point A to point B. For instance: All men are mortal, Bob is a man, and therefore, Bob is mortal.

Okay, logic got us to B, but what about the rest of the alphabet? And here, according to our genius friend, is where imagination takes us. Nothing lies beyond the reach of the mind unfettered by restrictions of logical thought. Imagination takes us to the edge of logic and allows us to roam freely in an atmosphere of unrestricted possibilities. It needs neither proof nor verification; or so seems to say the statement that we are discussing.

Granted, imagination has opened up the future. Western civilization is deeply indebted to those who were tired of recreating the wheel and dared to think of a more efficient alternative. We are grateful that Ben Franklin, among a multitude of other things, invented the lightning rod, the phonograph, the catheter, bifocals, the Franklin stove, the odometer, and played a crucial role in our understanding of the nature of electricity. Imagination, the Promised Land for pioneers in what might be.

The only caveat I would raise is that some things that could be, might better not be. While Einstein did not invent the atomic bomb, his insights were crucial to its development. Just five months before his death he said that the one great mistake he had made in life was to sign a letter to Pres. Roosevelt recommending that atom bombs be made (see Ronald Clark's book, *Einstein: The Life and Times*, pg. 754). My point is that imagination needs boundaries. It is not simply a harmless utopia but like all of life, a mixture of the good and bad. Whether or not the new possibility will benefit the human race is a moral decision. Without guidance we may well charge ahead into our own extinction. I know of no other set of moral directions more important to man, his nation, and the human race than God's revelation in Scripture. It lies behind the positive direction traditionally taken by Western civilization. May it guide us now and in the days ahead.

Losing what you don't have

ONE OF THE NEVER-ENDING questions in Christian circles is whether or not a believer can lose his salvation. Opposing camps of thought go all the way back to the early church. Verses can be carefully selected from Scripture that will "prove" either position. Once a decision has made, verses that seem to point to a different conclusion are swept under the exegetical rug. It is relatively easy to dispense with contrary evidence.

My position on the issue is relatively simple, "You can't lose what you don't have." Does that imply that you CAN lose what you DO have? And the answer to that depends on whether "losing" is up to you. I can lose my car keys because I am responsible to put them in the same place every night. If I don't, I will probably "lose" them, at least for a while.

But what if the responsibility for losing is not mine but someone else's? In that case I can still lose them but it won't be my fault. On the other hand, if the person responsible for my keys is absolutely reliable, unable ever to lose anything, then my keys are safe. But who can find a person who is absolutely unable to lose something. The answer must be God and if he is the one in charge of my keys then all is fine, he will never lose them.

So it comes down to this: If I am the one responsible for safeguarding my salvation, there is a real question as to how it will turn out. But if my salvation is in his hands, I can never lose it. But what about verses of scripture that seem to say rather definitely that one's salvation can be lost (I could gather the evidence but you would counter with verses that seem to say the opposite. So that isn't where the answer lies). If it turns out that my salvation gets lost, then all I can say is that I never had it. Back to my earlier maxim — "You can't lose what you don't have."

Will human nature ever change?

ONE OF THE INTERESTING things about human nature is that it seems never to change. A study of man over various periods of history shows that what we appear always to have been, we still are. Let's go back in history to about the seven century BC and listen to what the Jewish prophet, Jeremiah, had to say to his people. Israel had broken its covenant relationship to God and the "Weeping Prophet" warned the nation of an imminent destruction by the armored forces of Babylonia. What he revealed about human nature in his day is descriptive of life in the 21st century.

Looking at a single chapter in Jeremiah (chapter 8) we find that the people of Jerusalem are said to "cling to their deceit" (v. 5). Certainly, that describes the current situation in world affairs. I heard *Dr. O. Hobart Mowrer*, president of the American Psychological Association, once say that the major cause for mental disease is "man's duplicity." We have difficulty in presenting ourselves as we really are. I've been told that if we were to ask the inmates in a given prison if they were guilty as charged, we would discover not a single culprit. The ability to deceive oneself is a universal trait.

Further in the same chapter, Jeremiah, in reference to his people, notes, "None of them repent of their wickedness" (v. 6). To genuinely confess one's deviation from the acceptable norms of human behavior is rare. We often hear a public official who has been caught in an illicit affair say that he is "sorry that someone may have been offended." That is not a confession! Then the prophet adds that "each pursues their own course" (v. 6), "all are greedy of gain" (v. 10), and "they have no shame at all" (v. 12). Not a nice picture, but is it not true of the lower side of human nature?

Of course, that's not the whole story. The Christian faith also teaches that man was created in the "image of God." That means that there is also something about us that opens the prospect of a relationship with our Creator. In theology, the dark side is called "the fall of man." It is pictured in Scripture as an act of disobedience by the first couple. The Biblical story of redemption is that God, by the sacrifice of his Son, paid the price for sin and now offers forgiveness and restoration. So even though we are prone to live like we always have, there can be a bright future for those who turn to God in faith!

Why less is more

THIS IS THE QUOTE that caught my attention: "Media rearranges your values. It begins to dominate your life. And it has a profound impact on your attitude and outlook." It comes from "Becoming Minimalist," a website of *Joshua Becker* who, almost a decade ago, decided to put first things first and remove from his life all those pursuits that hindered his desire to center his life on the genuinely important.

Minimalism is normally thought of as doing without. Quite the opposite. It is removing that of secondary value so time and energy can be directed toward those things that are central to an authentic life. Quite some time ago my son reminded me, "What you own owns you." All the things that advertising boasts that you should have for a full and satisfying life create a vast clutter of unfulfilled desires bringing nothing but a sort of frantic sense of missing out in life. Minimalism offers a healthy alternative. Get rid of the burden of having more so that life can come into focus on the essentials. A deep satisfaction with the little that is central to living is infinitely more rewarding than the passing moments of narcissistic pleasure with abundance.

This train of thought got me thinking of Jesus. Everyone familiar with the story of his life is aware of how minimal was his need for material possessions. His disciple Matthew quotes him as saying, "Foxes have dens and wild birds have places to roost, but I have nowhere to lie down and rest, a place I can call my own" (Matt. 8:20). He told his disciples not to worry about what to wear or what to eat because God would take care of all that (Luke 12:22-32). If they would put God first and live righteous lives, he would provide them with all they needed (Matt. 6:33). That sure sounds like minimalism to me.

John D. Rockefeller is said to have replied to the question, "How much money does it to make a person happy," with, "One more dime." He many have been one of the richest men of his day but he knew that possession doesn't automatically equate to satisfaction. Since time itself is so limited wouldn't it be it wise to clear life of activities and pursuits that you know ahead of time yield no significant rewards? Every hour spent on a shallow and worthless TV program is an hour that could have been spent on something genuinely profitable and personally rewarding. It takes determination to put the best first but the reward is incredible. Here's to those who resist the lure of having for having's sake.

We need to be logical about logic

IN A RECENT ARTICLE, "Coming out of the Faith Closet," *Lynn Swayze Wilson* cites "the illogicality of the virgin birth" as one of the reasons for her conversion from Southern Baptist Christianity to Judaism. In her search for certainty she has found her home in Judaism. There were problems other than logic (for example, Evangelicalism's opposition to the kind of music associated with pop culture, a faith that excludes large numbers of people) but her journey away from Jesus to the "old G-d" (as she puts it) of Judaism seems to have begun with what she understood to be logical inconsistencies in the faith she inherited. Let's think about that.

There is no question that logic plays a central role in human thought and communication. We have no problem accepting the conclusion that if all boys like baseball and John is a boy then John likes baseball. That follows logically. So, is the virgin birth logical? Does it conform to the laws of reasoning? Well, that all depends (as we used to say). Are we talking about an issue that falls completely in a given realm (e.g., boys and baseball) or do we have a context that brings in something from beyond? For example: Philosophical naturalists cannot believe in the virgin birth because it would involve the action of a god, and for them god does not exist. The prior assumption rules out the conclusion.

But what about the supernaturalist who, by definition, assumes the existence of God? There is nothing illogical about God taking some action in his own creation. God is God and does what he pleases. All the Christian faith asks in regard to the virgin birth is that God be allowed to do something that, for all who believe in him, is perfectly logical.

The interesting point for me is that since God is in both Judaism and Christianity it would not be logical to allow him to part the Red Sea in the former, but deny him the power to effect a virgin birth in the latter. What would be reasonable in a conversion from Christianity to atheism (i.e., the rejection of Christianity on the basis of miracle) is unreasonable when it comes to a conversion between two religions, both of which assume the same God. Of course there were other reasons for Ms. Wilson's switch to Judaism, but a perceived lack of logic due to the miraculous in Christianity is a questionable base.

Remove morality and freedom disappears

C S LEWIS WROTE that "moral collapse follows upon spiritual collapse." Without a spiritual base, morality has neither guidance nor incentive. And I would extend the cause and effect process one more step: social collapse follows moral collapse. Our founders recognized that apart from morality there could be no free society. So where does that leave us? When the spiritual collapses so also does the moral followed by the social. Freedom is the final consequence of a morality that is based on man's relationship to God. Sever the spiritual and the end product is anarchy. The church exists as the salt of the earth, encouraging a morality that results in freedom. The current decline in morality (e.g., children born out of wedlock) is undermining our freedom. Time to get "salty" again.

Morality and freedom, inseparable twins

WE NEED TO REFLECT once again on *John Adam's* observation that "Our Constitution was made only for a moral and religious people. It is wholly inadequate to the government of any other." Why is that true? It's true because apart from a standard for what is right and wrong, the resulting "freedom" allows rebellious human nature to take control and chaos is the predictable result. Religion provides people with a set of rights and wrongs and if this moral code is removed there remains no particular reason for the individual to live in harmony with others.

In a morality free world nothing can be wrong — it's in the definition! If your neighbor decides to move his fence into your property, there's no reason why he shouldn't. The fence has been moved, you've lost land, but, since nothing is wrong, how could you argue that this was? I'm reminded of the story of an old VW van covered with stickers, one of which said, "If it feels good, do it." As it cruised along, a shiny new BMW pulled up behind wanting to pass. Reading the sign, the driver pushed the van off the road. The irate occupant of the van got out to protest, but found it difficult to deny that the other had the right to do whatever felt good to him. Gotta stick by your slogans!

At this point I'm not claiming that one set of responsibilities is necessarily better than another. All I'm saying is that apart from some standard, society cannot exist as such. What normally happens when a group of people moves away from regulation is that whoever has the power takes control. Now a standard does exist — the will of the most powerful. So, in fact, some sort of "morality" does exists. The crucial question is what sort of control is best? Which method of assuring the best for everyone has proven itself in history? The two extremes are absolute dictatorship at one extremity and the genuine freedom of social-concern at the other.

What Adams is saying is that apart from the control provided by an inward morality there is no way for freedom to flourish in a social setting. Our laws are simply secular expressions of our morality. We observe the speed limit because we don't want to endanger either ourselves or someone else. That people ought not drive faster than such and such a speed isn't an arbitrary decision. It's the result of a moral sense that driving too fast is wrong. Remove the moral element and freedom evaporates. True freedom is the opportunity to do what is right.

Riding bareback through life

I AM CERTAINLY HESITANT to comment on anything written by one of the greatest American poets, one who in his lifetime was awarded the Pulitzer Prize for Poetry four times. However, I am less critical than curious. *Robert Frost* wrote, "What is this talked-of mystery of birth but being mounted bareback on the earth?" At first I thought that by "mystery of birth" he was referring to the remarkable process whereby a fertilized egg becomes a living human being. Truly, that is a mystery. But then I sensed that he was using the word in a somewhat ironic sense — that is, while people normally refer to birth as a mystery, it is, in fact, no more than "being mounted bareback on the earth." If I understand him correctly, several questions arise.

The more we are learning about genetics and the nature of life, the more inscrutable the process becomes. In 2005 Melissa Moore wrote in Science Magazine that "Recent work indicates that the posttranscriptional control of eukaryotic gene expression is much more elaborate and extensive than previously thought." Okay, I don't know what that means, but what I do know is that each new advance in the field takes us onto a new level of complexity. Birth is a mystery — ask any mother holding a new born babe in her arms.

However, for some the period that follows, which we call life, may well be like "being mounted bareback on the earth." The figure suggests several things; first, vulnerability. If you have ridden bareback you know that should your horse suddenly spook right or left, there is very little to grab ahold of. I think that's why God gave the horse a mane. And life does have its sudden turns. One can never be sure that tomorrow will not bring a tragedy. Tornadoes happen and life on the highway is never secure.

But riding bareback also suggests exhilaration. It was my good fortune to have spent more than one summer on a reservation where, for five dollars, you could select a pony from the wild herd, brand it and it was yours. There is nothing quite like riding bareback out through the range, ridiculously happy to be alive and enjoying every moment. Can life be experienced that way? I believe so, although without an occasional siesta it might lose its thrill.

A good rider knows his horse, and they are all different. An Arabian is not a Quarter Horse. There are no Clydesdales in the Kentucky Derby. And life is like that. For some, the days and years go by with a regularity that creates the expectancy that tomorrow will be very much like today. But for others, life is a series of unexpected changes. Like a skittish horse, one never knows what might happen next. To have a good ride and arrive safely where we want to end up requires a knowledge of life. Horse and rider must cooperate. Scripture teaches that we were made for God and that he is our destination. It was a bad fall when Adam hit the ground (and we all suffer from his fatal choice) but Christ has made it possible to remount and arrive safely back at the ranch. Every good rider knows his horse, and those who trust life's Range Boss, even though once thrown, are back in the saddle and headed home.

Every law is a moral statement

APPARENTLY PEOPLE LIKE TO classify things. It makes life more manageable to get everything into categories. The biblical book of Proverbs lists "six things that the Lord hates, seven that are an abomination to him" (6:16-19). Christian ethics identifies the "seven deadly sins" as wrath, greed, sloth, pride, lust, envy, and gluttony. And Gandhi lists them as

- Wealth without works
- Pleasure without conscience
- Knowledge without character,
- Commerce without morality
- Science without humanity
- Worship without sacrifice
- Politics without principle.

Upon comparison you will find the three lists somewhat dissimilar. For instance, *Gandhi's* "questionable politics" is not included in Proverbs, whose "sowing discord" is not in Christian ethics, whose "gluttony" is not mentioned by the Hindu master. However the primary difference between the lists is that while the first two tell you *what* you are not to do, the third tells you *how* you are to do what you are free to do. So Proverbs lists things that the Lord hates (obviously implying that we should not do them) and Christian ethics warns against the seven deadly sins. These are things that should not be done. While Gandhi would probably agree with these negatives, he would rather state his ethical maxims more positively. Let's think about how we should live, not about what we shouldn't do. For instance, it's fine to have an abundance but use it for the benefit of others. Worship is good but it is designed to encourage sacrifice for others. Knowledge is good but apart from integrity it will not have a positive influence on society.

Note that Gandhi presents his seven deadly more as general principles than specific injunctions. He does not say, "Thou shalt not develop and use a poison gas against your enemies." While that would undoubtedly fall in his category of "science without humanity," it is simply a particular example of a moral principle. It is the principle that lies at the heart of the ethical system. To draw up an inventory of every possible example of how a principle might express itself would obviously be impossible. Far more effective is to teach the fundamental truth and expect the individual to learn how it applies in every aspect of life.

We consider ourselves to be a nation under law. But each individual law is an expression of a moral principle. "Speed limit 60" calls our attention to the fact that in that particular section of highway to travel at a faster rate is to risk the welfare of others. The speed limit is a "law" in the sense that it helps us understand what society feels is the proper speed so all will benefit. In a morally perfect world it would be unnecessary because everyone would live with welfare of the other in mind. In an ultimate sense, morality calls for dealing with social problems in terms of their underlying principles, not simply with how they might express themselves in particular situations.

Science and poetry, friends after all

It is interesting that what may be one of the best insights into the nature of poetry was written accidentally by a theoretical physicist. *Paul Dirac* noted that "in science one tries to tell people, in such a way as to be understood by everyone, something that no one ever knew before. But in poetry, it's the exact opposite." Science takes the mundane path of gathering data, discerning how they relate, and provide workable paradigms for the complexity of what we call reality. More simply, it tells people what they don't know in a way they can.

Then comes the claim that poetry is "the exact opposite." It tells people what they have always known in a way they can't understand. When I first read this I thought he meant that poetry begins with what we all know and then confuses us by stating it in a jargon no one recognizes. That is, science explains and poetry obscures. However, as I thought about, it may be that he said something very important about poetry. Another way of understanding what at first appears to be a negative regard for poetry, may well be the opposite. While science seeks to clarify, poetry uses a different language that invites us to go behind the obvious and see the "data" of life in a different way. Science explains for functional purposes, poetry "confuses" for artistic purposes. They are the "exact opposite" in method only. Both reveal truth but in two different ways and for two different purposes. Science is functional; poetry brings the larger context of life outside the test tube.

Certainly, both are necessary. Getting to the library calls for science. Experiencing meaning calls for metaphors outside the realm of science. Getting to the library is impossible apart from an understanding of our material world, but provides no reason why we should go there. Poetry attempts to provide insights into the "whys" of life.

Life's most practical GPS

THE OLD QUESTION, "IF you were stranded on a deserted island and could have only one book, what would it be?" has been answered in many ways. People's interest varies and it's hard to imagine what a given person might choose. We don't have to wonder about *Bernard Baruch*, however. This prominent American financier and statesman has already supplied the answer — *A Practical Guide to Boat Building*. Should he find himself on that deserted island he would do something about it; not read a book.

Minds run in different directions. Some are always in the land of make-believe. That's where difficulties are solved by deciding not to think about them but by embracing the unknown and pretending it's real. One military strategist during World War I is said to have recommended that the problem of German submarines could be solved simply by draining the ocean. When asked how that could be done, he said, "That's your problem; mine is theory." Society needs its dreamers but nothing would ever get done if the execution of the dream were left with them. Dreams don't come true without the doer.

A different mindset is to keep working until the perfect plan emerges. But this approach is bound to fail because it can never be fully realized. Time is spent researching the infinite complexity of the issue believing that the solution is just around the next corner. Quest for the perfect trumps the acceptable. So the theoretician redoubles his efforts to come up with the perfect answer. Life on the island, thinking about the perfect solution, is better than returning to the mainland.

The first decision to be made, if one's goal is to get from A to B, is to find out where B is. If the destination is not known, there is no road that will take you there. And this is the problem that surfaces again and again in life as we experience it. Our minds are distracted from what is genuinely important, so little or no time is spent on how we can get there. For the moment lets put Bernard Baruch on the island (his "A") wanting to get back to the mainland (his "B".) So how can he get there? His answer is straight forward — by building a boat, of course, and that requires a good book on how to build it. There's nothing quite as helpful as knowing how to get where you want to go. Pragmatism is the friend who drops by with the answer we should have thought about right away.

I believe that there is one "B" that's of ultimate importance. If B is heaven then the manual is God's Word. We are all on the same island and the vast majority of us would like to get back to the mainland, heaven. Fortunately we have the instructions detailed in Scripture.

Is our bright future behind us?

UPON COMPLETING HIS TWELVE-VOLUME analysis of the rise and fall of civilizations, *Arnold Toynbee*, the noted British historian concluded, "An autopsy of history would show that all great nations commit suicide." It would be difficult to find a single intellectual in the world today whose opinion on the subject would be considered superior.

Few would question that present day America provides an example of a nation in decline. The once bright spirit of hope for a better future is hard to find. There is general agreement that the next generation will not have it as good as we did. The college graduate no longer expects to move immediately into a well-paying job and a nice house in a pleasant neighborhood. Culture is moving 180 degrees from where we were forty or fifty years ago. Certain behavior that was lawfully judged as unacceptable is now celebrated as a significant moral advance. The time-honored role of marriage as a fundamental principle of organized society is now expanded to include relationships never imagined before. While for some this may be seem to be a step in the right direction, setting us free from the restricted environment of our Puritan heritage, for most it holds no real hope for the future.

Toynbee's use of the word "suicide" in this setting is interesting. It emphasizes that our descent is self-inflicted, not the result of some force outside our control. A nation rarely allows some other nation to determine its destiny. America is not the victim of China's rise in the economic world. We are not weaker because some other nation is stronger. We are doing it to ourselves. Our debt was not caused by the rising value of the Chinese yen but the unwillingness of leadership here at home to address our financial plight with honesty and integrity. Life today is a party on the Titanic!

We seem to believe that since we will soon be struggling in the icy waters of the North Atlantic we might as well finish off the champaign!

The only way to prevent one's own suicide is not to do it. It's that simple. I believe that if the people of our great land would understand what is happening, everything could be turned around. Small businesses, freed from unnecessary regulations, could be encouraged to expand. Individuals who have tried the alternative life-style and found it unrewarding could once again embrace the "faith of our fathers." There is a bright future behind us, but we will never get there if we continue in the wrong direction.

History has demonstrated the truth of Toynbee's thesis that nations commit suicide. Our responsibility as a nation is to decide, intentionally, whether he is right or wrong, and then to take appropriate action. There is time, you know.

Who is responsible for you?

"NOT IN THE CLAMOR of the crowded street, not in the shouts and plaudits of the throng, but in ourselves, are triumph and defeat" — *Henry Wadsworth Longfellow.* No one could have said it better. It all comes down to this, a person's true value has little or nothing to do with how others may or may not view him. Triumph is victory over self. Defeat is the recognition of personal failure. They are not dependent on the assessment of others.

Whether it is intentional or not, culture has a way of amassing people into various groups. The rock band electrifies the audience with its beat, gyrations, lights, costumes, etc. and thousands of young people press toward the stage, hands waving in the air, caught up in the ecstasy of the moment. Political issues are ultimately decided by which group produces the most effective bumper stickers. For many, worship is a group experience in which informed reflection on the Creator is replaced by an emotional reaction to so-called Christian music. This is not necessarily a criticism of those who are involved as it is an observation of how our life as unique individuals is being transformed into a part of some larger group.

The more I view myself as a member of a group the less personal responsibility I bear. I find my identity, as Longfellow put it, "in the clamor of the crowded street," enamored by "the shouts and plaudits of the throng." But that is not where we come to grips with the essential nature of life. We will move toward maturity as we recognize that we win or lose the battles of life on an individual basis. We are the ones who make the decisions crucial to life, not some crowd headed who knows where and accountable to no one.

Ultimately character is the end result of all our individual decisions. It is a final portrait of the countless brushstrokes of life.

Every act of kindness is there, mingled with every unkind word or deed. The beauty of the portrait depends entirely on the balance. Character is the legacy we leave for those still on the way. Worth serious reflection, is it not?

When greed is good

RECENTLY THE BRITISH ACTOR/COMEDIAN *Russell Brand* is on record as having said, "I say profit is a filthy word." Since I don't have the specific context in which this was said I am unable to agree or disagree. However, we can take what was said in a general sense and comment accordingly. A standard dictionary tells me that profit is the "pecuniary gain resulting from the employment of capital in any transaction." Less bookish it is "what you make from investing time or money."

That people are somewhat greedy animals cannot be denied. There are very few in this world that want less. The hermit is not the American model. We are pleased when our stock rises and rather discouraged when it suddenly drops. For some this concern borders on the pathological; for others it is simply a way of life. "Greed" cannot be eliminated by simply deciding it's wrong. It is too much of what it means to be a human being.

In most areas of human activity a moderate amount of what we are calling greed is essential for progress — not necessarily progress in the right direction, but progress. On July 2, 1962 Sam Walton opened a discount store in Rogers, AK and today it is the largest retail business in the world. Starbucks was founded in 1971 by three businessmen in Seattle, WA and today there are more than 20,000 Starbuck coffee shops around the world. Did greed have anything to do with successes like these? To get a Yes answer I believe you would have to change somewhat the standard definition of the word. Behind the vast majority of stories like these you will find an entrepreneurial spirit coupled with common sense and the willingness to work as hard as it will take.

I would like to think that this kind of "greed" is to some extent what has made America the remarkable country it is. Behind almost every success story there has been a basic desire to get ahead — economically as well as personally. What is wrong is not the desire for progress but the use of means that work to the distinct disadvantage of others. The successful salesman is not by definition unethical, but he is when he misrepresents his product for personal advantage. One of the distinct advantages of an open market is that this driving force has a way of putting restrictions on itself. Raise your price and people buy elsewhere. Provide substandard service and suddenly your profit drops. It may not be a lofty curb on greed but it seems to work.

No, profit is not a filthy word. Only when it is soiled by the desire to achieve at the expense of others. The fault is not in the exchange but in those who would manipulate it.

Scripture supports a balanced view of profit. On the one hand the Old Testament book of Proverbs teaches that "all hard work brings a profit" (Prov. 14:23), but the Israelites were told, "Do not take interest or any profit" from the "poor or those unable to support themselves."

The ultimate source of happiness

ADAM SMITH, BEST KNOWN for his classic, *The Wealth of Nations* once asked, "What can be added to the happiness of a man who is in health, out of debt, and has a clear conscience?" Certainly, no one can question the importance of good health, financial stability, and a clear conscience when it comes to judging quality of life. Many people have one of them, or perhaps two, but rarely do we find a person blessed by all three. Obviously, that person must be very happy? What could be "added to the happiness of a man" like that?

I'd like to think that while these three benefits are assuredly a genuine boon for a happy life, to suggest that nothing could be added (if Smith actually meant that) is hardly true. And I am not thinking of additional blessings of the same sort but of those that satisfy the deepest desires of the soul. So it may be well to pause and think about genuine happiness. What is a source of our greatest delight? What brings an ultimate sense of spiritual wellbeing? If we can answer that, then we will know what could be added to the good fortune of health, security, and a clear conscience. Jefferson suggested "tranquility and occupation," *Marcus Aurelius* said "the quality of your thoughts," and *Ayn Rand* knew it was "the achievement of values" (any good quote book will provide many more). All good, but will they meet our deepest desires? Will provide optimum happiness?

My sense is that while all these wonderful things may serve to provide pleasure in life, there is a fundamental reason why they ultimately fall short. As long as happiness is thought of as a goal it will always evade us. You can't be happy by trying. Happiness is result. It is a consequence not a goal. The "pursuit of happiness" may be well intentioned but you can't catch someone who is not in the race. So what is happiness?

At his point I have but two sources, the teaching of Scripture and personal experience — and it's important that they be kept in that order. The second, my experience of truth, is important for verification, but should never be the basis on which we judge something to be true. So I turn to Scripture and Jesus says, " I am come that they might have life, and that they might have it more abundantly (John 10:10). By faith I accept this as true and find that it is born out in life's experience. The abundant life, which Jesus supplies, maximizes the virtues recommended by Adam Smith and goes way beyond them. It certainly provides a clear conscience, for in Christ sin has been forgiven. It provides a debt-free life because it teaches the value of labor and removes the lust for more. It promotes good health because it teaches moderation in all things. All these bring a measure of happiness but fall short of our basic need, and that is to know God. No heart is at rest until it finds itself restored to God and that by a personal relationship with Jesus Christ. The pursuit of happiness must ultimately take us straight to the source of all happiness.

QBs gone west

ONE OF MY WALKS here in Anacortes, WA takes me to our little airport. As you enter the area there is a circle of benches around a metal table inscribed with the words, "To all QBs gone west." Obviously I asked myself, "What's a QB?" Certainly not a quarterback; there's no special connection between football and flight. So I Googled it and found it refers to a group of former pilots who formed the association in 1921. They call themselves the "Quiet Birdmen," the QBs. That some had "gone west" was not difficult to understand. They had reached the end of their years and died. The benches and table honored their contribution to life and the community.

We all "go west," that's for sure. "Three score and ten" has expanded to more like "four score and more" but regardless of the specific number, life comes to a close. Which makes us ponder. What's it all about? Is this all there is? Does it make a difference? The consistent materialist would say "Well, that's it! From the earth we came and to the earth we return. Any ideas about life beyond the grave arise from some vain hope that should there be more we'd like to be in on it. Understandable but outside of scientific certainty."

Fortunately many of us are unwilling to settle for the limited scope of the materialist. We recognize that scientific inquiry is limited to that part of reality you can measure. And you can't measure things like love, hope, friendship and desire. In fact, we instinctively accept the fact that much of what lies beyond the verifiable is what makes life worthwhile. We posit a realm that lies beyond. That which matches the deeper concerns of what it means to be alive.

The Christian faith begins with God. He is the Creator. He existed before he created. The universe that is carefully studied by the scientist is the gift of a creator God. Man, the ultimate act of God, has been created with a profound desire to know his Creator. And then comes "the rest of the story." In a moment of uncertainty man chose independence and it was granted. Now, apart from God, he wanders in a spiritual wasteland. Able to search out the intricacies of material reality he finds himself lacking the personal relationship intended by God. The answer is provided by a loving Father who gave his Son a sacrifice for man's sin.

This changes everything. Granted, we all "go west" but Scripture teaches that for those who in simple faith accept the saving work of the Father, west is heaven. May that be true not only for the QBs honored by the table engraved but for all whose final flight would take them into an otherwise hopeless eternity.

The timeless nature of a good quote

I HAVE ALWAYS LIKED a good quotation. It's not so much that it provides some new insight as it is that it captures an idea that has been wandering around in the periphery of one's mind and states it with clarity. There is a certain serendipitous quality to a good quote. It suddenly brings into focus what you have wanted to express. It elicits a strong Yes from beneath the surface of life. There is a certain timelessness about a good quote whether it is *Patrick Henry's* famous, "Give me liberty or give me death" or *Woody Allen's* farcical, " I am not afraid of death, I just don't want to be there when it happens." They make their point, there's no question about that.

Earlier, when I was writing on inspiration, I mentioned that O'Reilly had said that he had felt inspired to write *Killing Jesus*. I acknowledged that on a certain occasion, sitting at the piano and looking out over a gorgeous western sunset, I sensed that the descriptive phrases I wrote (now copyrighted) were not specifically mine. So when I happened to read *Andre Gide's* observation that "Art is a collaboration between God and the artist, and the less the artist does the better," I resonated with his observation. Obviously there is a contextual element in our evaluation of a quotation. What strikes us as brilliant in one situation may appear as slightly drab in another.

So, "Long live the good quote!" It brings focus to our thinking and often with charm. Quotations don't demand long periods of critical study before venturing a solution. One might say they are brash. But one thing is for certain, if they do not square with life as we experience it, they are quickly discarded. It was some 2,500 years ago that *Heraclitus* said, "Character is destiny," and not only do we remember this profound observation, but it has been repeated and applied in a myriad of ways from then forward. It is interesting that those issues that are central to the human species show up in the literature of every age. Technologically we have raced so far ahead that the ancient world is exactly that — ancient. But when we begin to consider such issues as love, hate, ambition, compassion, jealousy, anxiety, or desire, we find ourselves one with our predecessors. There's been little or no progress in that which is of ultimate importance. And that may be where the quotation comes in. A good quote is timeless because where we now are is where we have always been.

Time, the irreplaceable commodity

I THINK IT IS fair to say that some people seem always to be looking at what was (perhaps all do in the latter years), others are always looking forward, and still others simply do not look. *Charles F Kettering*, American inventor and businessman (he held 186 patents, founded Delco, and headed research at GM) definitely belongs in the second category. Without any desire to impress, he simply said, "My interest is in the future because I am going to spend the rest of my life there"

No one denies reality of death. It's as certain as taxes, as the old saying has it. Not many, however, spend much time talking about it. After all, it is a rather gloomy subject, sinister, and shrouded in darkness. But the future is not simply about death, but about all the incredibly valuable time between now and then. And that was what Kettering was talking about. To each individual has been allotted a certain amount of time to live and use for the benefit of others. The idea that life is for oneself is the plague of narcissism that has retarded the progress of civilization from the beginning. Even in the bounty of Eden's garden the first inhabitants decided that they knew better than God and that they should be the ones to reap any benefit there might be in an act of bold disobedience.

Time marches ahead with steady step and cannot be reversed. It refuses to go back. It lays out the framework for all that is yet to happen and invites the individual to invest his share of time in projects that reflect the goodness of the Creator and benefit the human race. I'm not talking about big enterprises in which the diligence of one generation enhances the life of the next. I am talking about little acts of kindness and concern that mirror in daily life the grace and goodness of the One who made it all possible. History has shown the value of altruism and the personal rewards of social concern. Like it or not we were meant for relationships and to allow selfishness to cheat us out of those rewards is a tragedy.

So, it is wise to use time carefully. Unlike a computer it doesn't "refresh," and once in "trash" it cannot be retrieved. Demonstrate by an other-oriented life the truth of Jesus' claim that to lose one's life is to save it (Luke 9:24).

Truth, the first casualty in war

IT WAS QUITE SOME time ago that *Mark Twain*, the American author and humorist, wrote, "If you don't read the newspaper you are uninformed; if you do read the newspaper you are misinformed." In 1910, the year of his death, television would have been considered a pipe dream. If he were writing today he would probably put it something like this, "If you don't watch TV you won't know whose dancing with the stars; and if you read the blogs you won't have the slightest idea what is true and what isn't."

I went to Snopes the other day to find out what they thought about a certain story circulating on the internet and discovered that over two-thirds of the material regarding the president was false. It seems as though once a person takes a position on a political issue, all evidence is regarded as true or false on the basis of whether or not it supports that opinion. What I am seeing is a breakdown of rational discussion, especially on issues of genuine significance. Someone said that "truth is the first casualty in war" and that is true both on the battlefield and in national debate. Facts are "true" only if they are helpful in winning one's point.

I am in no way hesitant to identify myself as a conservative. We conserve those things that have proven themselves over time. To bargain away what works for what might work is not a good idea. It is when what is said to work no longer works, that we look for better ways to accomplish the same goal. There is no problem with risking a failed procedure with a new one that holds promise. But to role the dice on life is no sign of intelligence or bravery. The question is, "Does our economic, social, and political system need a fundamental change"? A comparison with other systems around the world will lead the mature intellect to reject such an alternative. Does the existing system need tweaking? To be sure. "Fix it," not "Exchange it," should be our response.

The Value of Work

MY DAD WAS OF the opinion that boys belong on the farm so every summer during my early teens I was "farmed out" to some rancher in northern North Dakota. My pay was board and room. Several years later I earned $1 a day during harvest. Wow! In college I washed and waxed floors in several small stores down town Seattle. What did I make? I haven't the faintest idea. In any case it helped me make it through and get a degree from the university. I'm a Husky.

But did I, by any chance, get anything else for hours in the hot sun and for working on my knees at night? *Charles F Kettering* would say, Yes. He writes, "The highest reward for a person's toil is not what they get for it, but what they become by it." Well, I'm glad that $1 a day or proportionately more later on was not the full benefit. There were additional benefits that can be evaluated only over time. Here are a few:

I found that I could finish a job. Shocking grain is hard but shocking corn is even worse. The bundles are heavier and don't want to be moved. A cornfield looks awfully big to a boy of 14 responsible to shock the whole field. And the strings cut into young hands more used to playing the piano than dragging bundles around. But the farmer said, "Shock it" and the corn called out, "Come and get me," so there was nothing to do but go ahead and get it done. Fun ? Of course not. High monetary reward? Silly question. Any advantage for the boy? Yes. He learns that some things in this life simply need to be done and there is no easy way to get around it. Valuable lesson for a life still to be lived.

Here's another benefit for simply going ahead and doing it. You'll find it isn't as difficult as you thought it would be. How many pleasant experiences are missed by backing off just because something looked tedious? How refreshing to discover that there is an unexpected pleasure in doing what is necessary. A task is rarely as hard as you thought it would be. What is difficult is to get going. So don't judge how difficult something is until you've done it.

One more observation. As you take on the tasks of life you are building character. I know that sounds like a lousy reward, but it's true. A person is the sum total of all his decisions. Character is the final score — the only thing you take with you into the next world. You may have thought you had some things, but where are they now? "No pockets in a shroud," they say. But you do take with you what you really are, your character. That is "the highest reward for a person's toil." Ruskin was right.

Are we a dying society?

MOST PEOPLE, AS THEY grow older, spend an increasing amount of time thinking about years now gone past. It isn't necessarily that they have given up on the future, but that the past provides such a rich store of experiences that call for some sort of organization. Having reached my ninth decade, I find myself with one eye (the good one) on the future and the other on years gone past. My life has been spent primarily in higher education with research and writing in New Testament studies (since "retirement" it has been biblical translation.) While this has been highly rewarding, I sometimes wish I could have spent an equal amount of time becoming an expert in generalities. There is something about a good quote that pleases me. It brings clarity to confusion. It gives voice to an awareness I might have in some area but could never bring it quite into focus.

I had a colleague at the University, widely known for his expertise in genetics. The way he described advance in his area of science was something like this. Science begins with the accumulation of data. Upon observation a common thread emerges which seems to make sense — we call it a "law." Then additional data accumulates and our "law" enables us work more efficiently at a higher level and develop additional "laws." Or, as he put it, science is a process of simplifying complexity. But isn't that exactly what a good quotation does?

In the process of expanding our understanding we need a number of relatively secure generalities. No single one is without exception but that doesn't mean they are false. A generality that does not measure up to the test of time drops by the wayside. Why not have a division of advanced study dedicated to general statements rather than dedicating so much of our attention to finding out more and more about things that matter less and less?

Now the quote that got me started thinking along this line was *Aristotle's* observation that "tolerance is the last virtue of a dying society." As I apply this to the world in which I find myself, it strikes me as remarkably insightful. Certainly, as a nation, we are far more tolerant with the entertainment industry. I can still remember the shock of hearing Clark Gable's "Frankly, my dear, I don't give a damn." Tolerance has given us gyrations on a recent TV show that went beyond the burlesque of the thirties. Are we a "dying society?"

Leadership, always leaning left

I WAS STRUCK BY the relevance of something the prophet *Isaiah* wrote some 2,800 years ago regarding leadership. He predicted that in better days ahead "ungodly fools [would] not be heroes" (Isaiah 32:5). He writes that the social luminaries of his own day were "wealthy cheaters" who "spread lies," and "deprived the hungry."

But they were considered "heroes." That's what caught my attention. Why would people honor their oppressors with that designation? "Ungodly fools" belong in some sort of appropriate institution. They are a danger to society. But in Isaiah's days they were "heroes." Someone observed that the successful are distinguished by their achievements, celebrities by their image, but the hero creates himself.

I sense that throughout history every generation has allowed their "heroes" to lead. The hubris of these people far exceeds their ability but they manage their way into prominence anyway. But the story behind the story is the fatal lack of common sense of those who in every generation allow this to happen. Cultures decay and nations collapse because people are more interested in immediate pleasure and personal gain than in group stability and growth. Studies show that in every social group leadership is inevitably to the left of those being led. It ought to be obvious, then, why societies disintegrate and nations relegate themselves to the dustbin of history.

Why I believe in God

MIGUEL DE UNAMUNO WAS a Spanish intellectual whose philosophy was essentially negation. In his influential *The Tragic Sense of Life* he wrote that, in its essence, faith is "simply a matter of will, not of reason," and that "to believe in God is, before all and above all, to wish that there may be a God." As I understand this, it seems to say that faith is the decision to declare that God exists, totally apart from the support of reason or experience. If I may put words in his mouth, I hear him saying, "God is because I decide he is."

The first thought that crossed my mind was, that could hardly serve as an explanation for the universal belief in a higher power (a G/god). Even in the most primitive cultures, tribal groups have believed in a Supreme Being. 50,000 years ago the Neanderthal man buried his dead with ceremonies indicating a belief in life after death. I find it hard to believe that throughout time everyone (tribal native to contemporary man) who believed in god did so simply by "wish[ing] that there may be a God."

But let's not discard Dr. Unamuno's assertion without discussion. The basic question facing the average person is, how do I know there is a God? For me there are several parts to the answer. I believe I can reason effectively against the opposing viewpoint that God doesn't exist. God explains creation, supplies the reason and power behind what is. I have genuine trouble believing in a self-organizing world to say nothing of an accidental universe. Without God, one has to accept the eternality of matter and my mind can't manage that. Going the other direction, the intricacy of the cell argues a prior intelligence. Since the plan for life existed in the first living cell, isn't it reasonable to ask how the DNA got there? While reason doesn't prove God, it points us in that direction.

Second, I understand that people believing something for long periods of time doesn't prove it. Newton's universe fell apart as science moved ahead, but, as I mention above, the view that God (a higher power) exists has been central in human experience from the beginning. The human race could be wrong but let's give it the benefit of the doubt until reasonable alternatives arise.

Finally, I act on the assumption that God exists (more specifically for me, the God of the Judeo-Christian faith) and as a result I experience his reality. I remember visiting Christopher Wren's famous cathedral in London (St. Paul's) and when looking at its stained glass windows from the outside, being unimpressed. Then I went inside and the beauty of the morning sun breaking through those same windows took my breath away. Beauty is not ornamental but experiential. It is not so much in the object itself as it is in the response it elicits. When I entered the Christian faith by personal faith in Jesus the windows of heaven displayed both beauty and reality. I could never have experienced that from without.

Is there a God? How does one know? To summarize the above: Think about it, reflect on it, and experience it. I know of no more persuasive way.

Seeing what isn't there . . . yet

FOR THE MOST PART, we simply react to life. Days come and go and we handle each one pretty much as we always have. The prospect of turning life into an adventure, by looking more deeply into the events of each day, escapes us. Life has lulled us into conformity. We have come to know how the "group" handles each kind of experience and the tendency to surrender to banality is strong.

But there is an alternative. It is vision. In every event of life there is something that escapes the eye of the vast majority. However, every now and then comes along a visionary whose mind goes beyond the obvious and sees something totally different. *Jonathan Swift* identified vision as "the art of seeing things invisible." The invisible is what could be. The normal eye sees a run-down house in a poor area of town. Vision sees the house renovated, adorned with flowering shrubs and hanging plants and open as a historic cottage now a bed and breakfast. The normal eye saw nothing but an awkward row of buttons. Vision saw a better way of closing a jacket and after eleven years of rejection by various companies (true story) produced the zipper.

Every profitable business, every successful community organization, every significant national advance is the result of vision. So why isn't this better way of seeing — seeing what isn't yet there — taught in our schools? It could be argued that only a few have the unique ability to see the invisible. I don't think so. I believe that curiosity is a trait born into every individual. We see so little of it in practice because it is stifled by groupthink. "Go along to get along" is the mantra that stifles ingenuity in every area. Failure to see beyond the obvious robs every individual of a pleasure that belongs to all.

So look around. Look within. Survey the incredible world in which we live. Marvel at the complexity of the human body. Think about what could happen in any segment of society. Look for the invisible. I predict it will emerge out of the mist that normally keeps us from seeing what could be.

Is there someone "outside the barrel?"

THE HUMORIST, *MARK TWAIN* had a way of making his point with a rare mix of insight and wit. What he says tends to linger, not simply because it strikes us as true, but also because it brings a smile. For instance, "The two most important days in your life are the day you are born and the day you find out why." Obviously one's first day is important because apart from it we wouldn't be here. To acknowledge the obvious has its own way of amusing the mind.

But what about finding out why you are here? Most would agree that that should be an important day. Unfortunately that day has not as yet arrived for so many who have never taken the time to consider the question. If you think the WHY question is important then what follows may be of interest.

Everyone has a worldview. It is your framework of belief through which you interpret the world and interact with it. More simply it is the way you view reality. Now comes the crucial question, "Is there a God?" Everything else depends upon this answer. If you believe that the universe was created, then you necessarily acknowledge a prior being or force. If you rule out such a possibility then you are a materialist. Each basic presupposition requires an act of faith because neither can be proven or disproven. In his well-known book, *Miracles*, C S Lewis' pictures some fish in a barrel, swimming around and enjoying life. They believe that nothing exists outside that barrel. One day a boy passing by drops a stone into the water and little ripples cover the surface. Now the fish are faced with a serious intellectual problem: either it didn't happen or something must exist outside the barrel. I find myself with the "supernatural" fish. I believe there is something/someone outside the universal barrel. From the basic premise of a creator God I construct a worldview that answers the problem of human existence better than any alternative. (I highly recommend James Sire's book, *The Universe Next Door*.)

So why is it important to "find out why" you are here? The Christian world-view tells us that life is a moral experience and extends into an eternal realm; therefore it is important to make that transition correctly. It goes on to teach that God made the right transition possible by giving his Son as a sacrifice for sin and offering forgiveness to all who will accept him by faith. Final proof awaits fulfillment, but in the meantime God grants the assurance not only of his own existence but of the truth of what he is telling us.

It's called "semantic range"

Eugene Nida, the widely known linguist who developed the translation principle known as dynamic equivalence, once said that language is a "dictionary of fading metaphors." Nida was at the forefront of a movement in linguistics that focused on what was being translated rather than the words used for the task. Even when we refer to a tangible object like, say, a "table," the term may have a surprising breath of meaning: we normally eat on one, actions unknown to others are said to be under it, we use it to postpone discussion on an issue, it describes an abbreviated list, etc. When we move into the less tangible realm we find ourselves even less secure. Take the word "fast." You can run that way, it describes the period of time when you choose not to eat, it's used of colors that don't fade, it describes young people who disregard moral conventions, etc.

In what sense is a word a "fading metaphor?" Every word serves to represent an object, a sensation, an action, an idea, etc. With use, its semantic range is extended. The original rather crisp image fades and now serves in a number of somewhat similar contexts. As words extend themselves they become increasing less precise. No longer strong, they lose their excitement.

Language is a remarkable gift to the human specie. From a scientific perspective, the ability of Homo sapiens to communicate at sophisticated levels   is one major thing that distinguishes them from other mammals. Of the some 6,800 spoken languages in the world, it is said that English has the largest vocabulary. Google scanned 15 million English-language books and came up with 1,013,913 as the vocabulary number as of January 1, 2012. And we have been adding 14.7 words per day ever since.

So language is both expanding and fading. We have more and more words but those words are losing their impact. This poses no particular problem for ordinary life but it does create a serious problem for translating an ancient language. The tendency is to read more into a word that was intended at the time the word was first spoken or written.

It is not that people can't understand one another adequately. What I am suggesting is that in view of the above considerations, one ought to use language judiciously. Assuming that a person wants to be clearly understood, clarity and simplicity are the rules of the game. A commitment to integrity in language will make a difference for our nation because it is the means for the free exchange of ideas.

Why we are like we are

FROM TIME TO TIME I have said that my purpose in this blog is to reflect upon various quotations that have piqued my curiosity and do it from a Christian world-view. At this point it may be helpful to say something about that term since it originated in another culture. World-view is the English equivalent of the German Weltanschauung (from Welt, world, and Anschauung, perception). The World English Dictionary defines Weltanschauung as "a comprehensive view or personal philosophy of human life and the universe." It is a way of looking at the totality of human existence here on planet earth. It is our perception of reality.

When I say Christian world-view I am asserting that the Christian faith, based upon God's self-revelation in Scripture, has a specific way of looking at what is. For example, it holds that God created the world and thus differs from the philosophical materialist who claims no knowledge of how matter came about but is sure that nothing else exists. This is not an insignificant difference. The fact that a supernatural being exists carries the strong possibility that life here on earth brings with it some sense of obligation. If, on the other hand, what is, is simply a normal development in the material realm, then it would be hard to understand why I ought to do this instead of that. The Christian world-view holds very distinctly that man's obligation is to conform to the expectations of his Creator. A world-view that posits God wants to live in a way that will please him. If there is no God, there is no one to please.

One of the areas that exhibit the superiority of the Christian world-view is social responsibility. Fifty some years ago President Johnson launched the war on poverty. Over $16 trillion has been spent and the percentage living in poverty now is roughly the same. Why is that? The Christian world-view proposes care for the widow and orphan (James 1:27) but also says, "The one who is unwilling to work shall not eat" (2 Thess. 3:10). If everyone would take that seriously, the situation would change dramatically.

Another area where world-view makes a difference is the nature of man. Nothing explains the conflicting qualities of ego-centricity and nobility as well as the Biblical teaching that man is made in the image of God (has certain qualities that reflect the nature of God) yet by a sinful choice to go it on his own (the fall in Eden) has allowed sin to control his actions. He will dive into the raging stream to save child yet live out his days in selfish concern for what is best for him.

World-views are not provable. They lie outside reason's domain. But there are ways to satisfy the responsible person that some ways of thinking about life are better than others. The theologian/philosopher John Edward Carnell used to say that one set of presuppositions is preferable to another if (1) they are inwardly consistent, and (2) they answer better to life as one experiences it. On that a basis, I am confident that the Biblical approach to understanding mankind (specifically, why we do what we do) is far superior to all competing views.

Be wise about what you know

SOCRATES HELD THAT THE only thing he knew was that he knew nothing. "There is a deep insight in this," comments *A C Grayling,* "for the one thing that is more dangerous than true ignorance is the illusion of knowledge and understanding."

Two things strike me as the years roll by — how much there is that could be known and how little of it I know. Like most young men in their late teens or early twenties I thought I knew pretty much everything required for a normal life. Confronting a problem, I was confident that with a few minutes to check it out I would have the answer (and that was before ask.com or the dozen or so rapid answer sites available on the Internet). Then I chose a profession and began to learn a lot more in a specific area. My specialty was New Testament studies. I learned Koine Greek, understood the complementary infinitive, wrote a paper on Judas Maccabaeus, and after thirteen years of careful study, a critical commentary on John's Apocalypse. Now that took time. Had I pursued history, I would have learned an entirely different set of facts, or had I gone to medical school (as I had planned) I would now know a lot more about the human body. What strikes me is that competence in one area needs to be understood as part of a larger context. A genuinely wise person will take what he knows in his specific area and relate it to the real world in which he finds himself.

Someone said that academic research involves learning more and more about less and less until everything is known about nothing. I don't mean to discredit research in fields that are beneficial to society (e.g., cancer research, robotics, etc.), but the assumption that extensive knowledge in one narrow field provides expertise for knowledge in the broader sense is invalid. Most learned people, if they are also wise, recognize the vast extent of information that exists in an infinite number of fields. And if that is true of what is now known, think of all that will be known. The first cave man to learn how to make fire was the intellectual genius of his day. So what of today's intellectual giants? From the perspective of tomorrow's knowledge, they join the celebrated ranks of cavemen of yesterday. And that is not a put down, just a call for trans generational modesty.

My grandmother taught school from the age of 17 until she arrived at 70. Nothing pleased her like learning. She was interested in everything. Her view of heaven was learning forever. Always wondered about that during school days but now I am beginning to catch on how wise she really was.

Power, the political aphrodisiac

LIN YUTANG, THE INFLUENTIAL Chinese writer, noted that "when small men begin to cast big shadows, it means that the sun is about to set." We know that great men cast big shadows and nations are blessed by the impact of their lives and the legacies they leave. But there are also small men who cast big shadows and society is left in shambles. History has a way of producing its fair share of Hitlers, Stalins, Pol Pots, and Kim Jong-ils and they all cast enormous shadows. As the sun goes down, millions are adversely affected by their reigns.

There is no question but there are plenty of big men in this world — good men who are living out their days in a fair and honorable way. They pay their taxes, get along with their neighbors, work hard, raise good kids, contribute to charity, etc. Then why do "small men" seem so oft en to be in charge? What is there about power that attracts? Christian theology teaches that man (and I uses the word genetically) is a creature made in God's image but flawed by disobedience. The result is universal narcissism. Power is the political aphrodisiac that all too often draws the unqualified into public office. Plato was right when he said, "One of the penalties for refusing to participate in politics is that you end up being governed by your inferiors." What a nation needs in positions of leadership are good men able to resist the corrupting influence of power.

Friendship, the result of sharing

"SHARED JOYS MAKE A friend, not shared sufferings," *Friedrich Nietzsche*. I had to think about this one for a while. Certainly "shared joys" make a friend. I can still remember a university buddy who was handicapped (couldn't walk, some strange neurological problem) and had to be carried. I was his number one source of transportation and had him on my back for two years. Every now and then we would double date and I would carry him on my back downtown Seattle on the way to a cinema. When people took more than a casual look at us he would point down at me, grin and say, "He lost the bet!" Jack was a special friend and all our good times together strengthened that relationship. When he died in the 80s his family hung a huge sign in the window that read, *He's walking!!*

But what about "shared sufferings?" I've had those as well. In my experience they have played pretty much the same role. I could describe some but they're too personal to relate in this setting. It wouldn't be fair. But let me recount how they affected me. First, I can't imagine the suffering of a friend that wouldn't draw me closer to him. I would want to be one with him in his difficulty and help in any way I could. As we travelled through the difficulty we would share the joy of having endured it together and found relief and joy at the other end. When we celebrated deliverance I'd be the first to raise a toast

For the Christian there are several verses of Scripture that speak of the joy of shared suffering. In Romans 8:17 the apostle Paul writes to the church in Rome that if they "share in [Christ's] sufferings," they will also "share in his glory." The suffering to which Paul refers is the opposition of others to the message of the crucifixion of Christ (ranging all the way from social avoidance to martyrdom.) Experience convinces me that difficulties like that strengthen my friendship with God. Today is Pearl Harbor day and the news media report that survivors of that tragedy often have their ashes returned and buried under water in the USS Arizona so they can be with their buddies who went down with the ship. Isn't that a great example of shared suffering building a lasting friendship?

It's remarkable that friendship can be the product of two opposite kinds of experiences — shared joys and shared suffering. The point is that friendship is the fruit of sharing and it doesn't matter whether the experience is good or bad. No doubt about it, we were made for one another!

Index of subjects

Index of subjects

People quoted

Adams, John
Angelou, Maya
Aristotle
Asimov, Isaac
Baruch, Bernard
Becker, Joshua
Beecham, Sir Thomas
Brand, Russell
Camus
Cousins, Norman
Crooks, James
Cuban, Mark
Dalai Lama
Dirac, Paul
Dostoevsky
Dr. Phil
Einstein, Albert
Eisenhower, Dwight
Eliot, George
Frost, Robert
Gandhi
Gide. Andre
Glasgow, Arnold H.
Grayling, A. C.
Hemingway. Ernest
Hepburn. Audrey
Holmes, Oliver Wendell
Isaiah
Kahneman,
Kennedy, John
Kettering, Charles F.
La Harpe, Jean Francois de
Lewis, C. S.
Lin Yutang

Longfellow, Henry Wadsworth
Marx, Groucho
Mencius
Mowrer, Dr. O. Hobart
Nida. Eugene
Nietzsche, Friedrich
O'Reilly, Bill
Orwell, George
Plato
Rand, Ayn
Rockefeller, John D.
Smith, Adam
Socrates
Sowell, Thomas
Swift, Jonathan
Tebow, Tim
Tennyson. Alfred Lord
Thatcher, Margaret
Twain, Mark
Unamuno, Miguel de
Vauvenargues, Marquis de
Voltaire
Washington, George
Wayne, John
Weber, Max
Wells, H. G.
Wilde, Oscar
Wilson, Lynn Swayze
Yeats, William Butler

Made in the USA
Coppell, TX
05 February 2020

15386042R00085